SISTERS' LIBRARY
MOTHERHOUSE

HOLY
SATURDAY

D0107484

HOLY SATURDAY

AN ARGUMENT FOR THE
RESTORATION OF THE FEMALE DIACONATE
IN THE CATHOLIC CHURCH

PHYLLIS ZAGANO

A Herder & Herder Book
The Crossroad Publishing Company
New York

The Crossroad Publishing Company
370 Lexington Avenue, New York, NY 10017

Copyright © 2000 by Phyllis Zagano

All rights reserved. No part of this book may be reproduced, stored in a retrieval system, or transmitted, in any form or by any means, electronic, mechanical, photocopying, recording, or otherwise, without the written permission of The Crossroad Publishing Company.

Printed in the United States of America

Library of Congress Cataloging-in-Publication Data
Zagano, Phyllis.
    Holy Saturday : an argument for the restoration of the female
diaconate in the Catholic Church / Phyllis Zagano.
        p. cm.
    Includes bibliographical references and index.
    ISBN 0-8245-1832-2
    1. Deaconesses – Catholic Church.   I. Title.
BX1912.2 .Z34 2000
262'.142'082 – dc21
                                        00-008201

1   2   3   4   5   6   7   8   9   10   06   05   04   03   02   01   00

For all the women of the Church

Then Yahweh answered me and said:
"Write the vision down,
inscribe it on tablets to be easily read.
For the vision is for its appointed time,
it hastens toward its end and it will not lie,
although it may take some time, wait for it,
for come it certainly will before too long...."
— *Habakkuk 2:2–3*

Contents

Prologue ix

Part One: PREPARING THE ARGUMENT............1

The Church must formalize the ministry of women.

Part Two: THE ARGUMENT.......................21

*The restoration of the female diaconate is necessary
for the continuance of the apostolic life and ministry
of the Roman Catholic Church.*

   I. Men and women are ontologically equal. 22

  II. The Church has given reasons why women, although 36
      ontologically equal to men, may not be ordained
      to priesthood.

 III. The judgment that women cannot be ordained priests 64
      does not apply to the question of whether women can be
      ordained deacons.

 IV. Women are and have been called to the diaconate. 73

  V. There are stronger arguments from scripture, history, 87
      tradition, and theology that women may be ordained
      deacons than that women may not be ordained deacons.

 VI. Women have continually served the Church in diaconal 111
      ministry, whether ordained to such service or not.

VII. The ordained ministry of service by women is necessary 133
      to the Church, that is, to both the People of God and
      the Hierarchy.

Part Three: CONCLUSIONS 167

The ordination of women to the diaconate is possible.

Index 175

Prologue

Today is Saturday. Today, this year, this decade, this century is the Saturday the women waited faithful, trusting, loving, having seen what really happened, and knowing how and why they could not abandon the promise they had heard, that they believed. Today is that same Saturday, as nations war and power once again takes precedence over person. Today we face the same split within and without, between the world of the spirit and the temporal world, between the New Jerusalem and Babylon, between the powerful and the powerless. Today is that same Saturday, when the old must accommodate the new, not replacing but complementing and strengthening the truths of God's revelation. Today is Holy Saturday, filled with hope.

PART ONE

PREPARING THE ARGUMENT

The Church must formalize the ministry of women.

❖ ❖ ❖

This discussion is aimed at supporting the needs of the Church.

Church is a living reality made possible by the Easter that followed Holy Saturday. This work is meant to bring us to another Easter in the Church, one when women will minister in a new and an old way, as ordained deacons. It is an argument constructed in love and in hope, but one that acknowledges some of the anger among women in the Church. It is not a separatist argument, though it recognizes that separatism exists. It is rather an argument to help the whole Church rediscover its past and understand a reality already present.

This work, therefore, is an attempt to expand what Pope John Paul II has called for: deeper and more meaningful "feminine participation in every way in [the Church's] internal life." John Paul II continues:

> This is certainly not a new commitment, since it is inspired by the example of Christ himself. Although he chose men as his Apostles — a choice which remains normative for their successors — nevertheless, he also involved women in the cause of his kingdom; indeed, he wanted them to be the first witnesses and heralds of his resurrection. In fact, there are many women who have distinguished themselves in the Church's history by their holiness and hardworking ingenuity. The Church is increasingly

1

aware of the need for enhancing their role. Within the great va-
riety of different and complementary gifts that enrich ecclesial
life, many important possibilities are open to them. The 1987
Synod on the Laity expressed precisely this need and asked
that "without discrimination women should be participants in
the life of the Church, and also in consultation and the process of coming to decisions" (*Propositio* 47; cf. *Christifideles Laici,*
no. 51).[1]

The Pope makes a serious call to meet a serious need. Women
clearly are not well-integrated into the Church's structure, primarily because even offices that may be filled and ministries that
may be performed by women are provided or assigned to women
only when a qualified man is not available. Hence, it is no secret
that a goodly number of the women of the Church are unhappy
with it. Tensions rest in women's refusal to accept the residual
notion that only a man is created in the image and likeness of
Christ. There is too much evidence that Christ did not abide by
such barriers, too much evidence that he stretched his culture
as far as he could, too much evidence that his stretching was in
fact retracted. The Pope, in his allocution on women's role in the
Church, further stated:

> This [the inclusion of women in ecclesial life] is the way to be
> courageously taken. To a large extent, it is a question of making
> full use of the ample room for a lay and a feminine presence
> recognized by the Church's law. I am thinking, for example, of
> theological teaching, the forms of liturgical ministry permitted,
> including service at the altar, pastoral and administrative coun-
> cils, Diocesan Synods and Particular Councils, various ecclesial
> institutions, curias, and ecclesiastical tribunals, many pastoral
> activities, including the new forms of participation in the care
> of parishes when there is a shortage of clergy, except for those
> tasks that belong properly to the priest. Who can imagine the
> great advantages to pastoral care and the new beauty that the

---

[1] John Paul II, "Women's Role in the Church" (September 3, 1995), in *Pope John Paul II on the Genius of Women* (Washington, D.C.: United States Catholic Conference, 1997, 1999), 35.

Church's face will assume, when the feminine genius is fully involved in the various areas of her life?[2]

The Pope's hopeful words address a serious situation. Not only is there a shortage of persons committed to the pastoral care of souls, the lack of women in leadership roles in the Church sends mixed signals to the whole Church, and beyond, to the world it expects to evangelize. It is a painful reality that there will be little progress, not only for women in the Church or for women with the Church, but also for the whole task of evangelization, until the role of women in the Church is clarified.

There are inherent systemic difficulties.

A substantial cause of the difficulty of "making full use of the ample room for a lay and a feminine presence recognized by the Church's law" is the resistance offered by a solely male and predominantly celibate male clerical system. This system does not easily allow for ordinary professional relations between its members and the rest of the Church, and especially between its members and women. Clearly, the underlying difficulty of the ordinary relations between the sexes in professional Church work must be resolved. The real needs of the People of God cry out for such resolution, as the Catholic bishops of the United States have well recognized:

> The face of the Church reveals the pain that many women experience. At times this pain results from the flawed behavior of human beings — clergy and lay — when we attempt to dominate each other. Women also experience pain because of persistent sexism. At times this sexism is unconscious, the result of inadequate reflection. A Church that is deepening its consciousness of itself, that is trying to project the image of Christ to the world, will understand the need for ongoing, prayerful reflection in this area.[3]

---

[2]John Paul II, "Women's Role in the Church," 35–36.

[3]National Conference of Catholic Bishops, *Strengthening the Bonds of Peace: A Pastoral Reflection on Women in the Church and in Society* (Washington, D.C.: United States Catholic Conference, 1995), 11. This document was developed by the Committee on Women and

Such a "persistent sexism" has been institutionalized by default in a system that prefers men to women specifically by preferring those in clerical orders to those not in clerical orders, and by not allowing women to become clerics.

It is truly an uncomfortable fact that many people simply do not take the Church seriously, and part of the lack of credibility is a cognitive dissonance between what the Church apparently teaches and that which it in fact practices. That is, the dignity of the married state and its equality to virginity, and the equality of all, male and female, are fully discussed in Church documents but not symbolized by membership among the Church's clerics. This is not to say that ministry by male clerics (married or celibate) is ineffectual, for such is not the case. It is simply to point to the variegated pattern of the Church as the body of Christ, and the need for its ordained ministry to better mirror the People of God. Despite the growth of the permanent diaconate, the Church is still perceived as controlled by celibate men. But if the Church is to present itself as witness to Christ in the unfolding century, it might well examine its own understanding of the various talents it has within it and recognize that the varied talents of varied people can be used to argue more strongly for its tenets.

An argument for women's ordained ministry addresses the needs of the Church.

This book comprises an argument for the restoration of the fe-male diaconate in the Roman Catholic Church as a response to the needs of the Church, both as an evangelizing reality and an organizational bureaucracy. The analysis and argument presented here is intended to speak to the principal unity required of all Christians who are believers in the power of God through the Church as established by Christ. The effort here is to think *with* the Church, and in fact with the "hierarchical Church," as it has come to be called, as well as with the People of God. It is therefore

Society and in the Church and approved by the Catholic Bishops of the United States at their general meeting in November 1994.

an effort to think along with the Magisterium, as it reflects the Spirit's movement in the whole Church.

There is a need for a "hierarchical Church" as an organizing and bureaucratic reality, which should be understood as a theological reality. In these pages, however, the term "Church authority" replaces "hierarchical Church" as the conveyer of the Magisterium.

Whether "Church authority" or "hierarchical Church," the reality denoted is at odds both with secularism and with a secular faith in its bureaucracy. The International Theological Commission noted that "secularism, in the radical sense, excludes every idea of Church as a hierarchical structure."[4] That is, secularism finds the world in and of itself an idol, and as a closed system it rejects the transcendent to an ultimate rejection of all authority, but especially of ecclesial authority. Beyond and by deduction, then, neither must there be a "secular faith" in the structure of the Church as structure. The Church is both human and divine. As a human institution it has flaws past and present, but these do not affect the deposit of faith except insofar as they are contravening attitudes to basic teachings. To create an idol of a structure is such a contravening attitude. Hence, the living faith requires a living structure, capable of change.

In no way does this argument for change counter the Magisterium. Rather, it intends to point a way by which women can continue to serve the Church in union with Church authority if the whole Church, on behalf of the People of God, will return to ordination as a means of formalizing the ministry of women.

Once established, the argument presented here moves from analysis of the ontological equality of men and women to the present teachings relative to ordination of women to priesthood, which do not apply to the questions surrounding diaconal ordina-

---

[4]"The Priestly Ministry" in Michael Sharkey, ed., *International Theological Commission: Texts and Documents 1969–1985* (San Francisco: Ignatius Press, 1989), 18, fn. 16. "Secular faith and hierarchical authority exclude each other. Consequently, the Church of the future must differ from what it has been in the past." J. Sperna Weiland, *La nouvelle théologie* (Paris: Desclée de Brouwer, 1969).

tion for women. Then, the diaconal service of women is examined, including evidence from scripture, history, tradition, and theology. The continued service of women in diaconal roles supports the final point, that the ordained ministry of service by women is necessary to the Church. The argument's conclusion is that the ordination of women to the diaconate is possible.

The Church's categories create a separatism.

The question of whether the Church is a participatory democracy is one raised often by Americans who recognize more the political analogies of Church than the eschatological realities of *ecclesia*. There is no attempt in this work to create a democratic principle for moral or doctrinal argument, despite work that is a precursor to a call for such experimental democracy in what is coming to be known as "The American Catholic Church."[5] The present case asks that the Church make better use of its own people if it is to serve them through belief in Christ, independent of the political exigencies of a given nation. The Church is, in fact, in clear danger of becoming a congregationalist, nonsacramental entity by default.

The Church's teaching, sanctifying, and governing needs are met primarily by ordained males. The Church needs more workers. Obviously, the Church carefully guards its heritage, and in its wisdom it does have means by which the nonordained can in fact share in the teaching, sanctifying, and governing roles usually restricted to clerics.[6] But clergy form the core of those who teach, sanctify, and govern. It would not be helpful, therefore, to see the

---

[5]See especially Dennis P. McCann, *New Experiment in Democracy: The Challenge for American Catholicism* (Kansas City, Mo.: Sheed & Ward, 1987).

[6]Canon 766 provides for lay preaching "if in certain circumstances it is necessary" and references Canon 767, which reserves homilies during mass to priests and deacons. At present, lay persons properly deputized can administer baptism (Canon 861) and witness marriages (Canon 1112). In these cases, women religious are considered lay persons. References to the Code of Canon Law are to *Code of Canon Law, Latin-English Edition*, trans. Canon Law Society of America (Washington, D.C.: Canon Law Society of America, 1983). This code was promulgated by John Paul II on January 25, 1983, following a revision process begun in 1965, which included circulation of drafts of specific sections throughout the 1970s. This second Code of Canon Law replaced the 1917 Code, which ceased to bind on November 27, 1983.

rich and varied possibilities for lay ministry as replacing the need for ordained women.

At the outset, it is well to recognize that there is some confusion relative to terminology. *Lumen Gentium,* the Dogmatic Constitution on the Church published by the Second Vatican Council in 1964, uses the term "lay" in two distinct and seemingly contradictory ways. In the first use, in chapter 4, "The Laity," "lay" refers to all persons who are neither clerics nor religious:

> The term "laity" is here understood to mean all the faithful except those in Holy Orders and those who belong to a religious state approved by the Church. That is, the faithful who by Baptism are incorporated into Christ, are placed in the People of God, and in their own way share the priestly, prophetic and kingly office of Christ, and to the best of their ability carry on the mission of the whole Christian people in the Church and in the world.[7]

In the second use, in chapter 6, "Religious," "lay" is used as distinguished from clerical:

> [Religious life] . . . has its own place in relation to the divine and hierarchical structure of the Church. Not, however, as though it were a kind of middle way between the clerical and lay conditions of life. Rather it should be seen as a form of life to which some Christians, both clerical and lay, are called by God so that they may enjoy a special gift of grace in the life of the Church and may contribute, each in his own way, to the saving mission of the Church.[8]

The result of these disparate uses creates a sense of three separate types of persons: the cleric (a member of the clergy), the religious, and the lay person, or laic. In terms of Canon Law, and certain

---

[7]*Lumen Gentium,* no. 31. This use is not consistent with the Code of Canon Law, 207, which distinguishes between sacred ministers, or clerics, and other Christian faithful, or laity, but is consistent with the Code of Canons for the Eastern Churches, Canon 399, which defines "lay" as all those neither in orders nor enrolled in the religious state.

[8]*Lumen Gentium,* no. 43, citing Canons 487 and 488.4 (of the 1917 Code); Pius XII, Allocution "Annus Sacer" (December 8, 1950), *Acta Apostolicae Sedis* 43 (1951): 27; Pius XII, *Const. Apost. Provida Mater* (February 2, 1947), *Acta Apostolicae Sedis* 39 (1947): 120.

Conciliar and later documents, the tripartite separation is correct: "clerics" and "religious" are specific categories for whom special accommodations are made, and "the laity" is everyone else. But when "cleric" or "clergy" is placed in apposition with "laic" or "lay," even within religious life, the distinction is only between those ordained and not ordained.[9] That is, the rights and duties of clerics do not accrue to religious unless those religious are ordained. In the case of women religious, all are lay, and hence their ministry is restricted along with that of any other lay person. Note that Pope John Paul II pointed to *Christifideles Laici* in commenting on the need to increase the role of women in the Church.[10]

The very title of the 1994 Synod on Consecrated Life[11] indicated an expansion of the term "religious" with the use of "consecrated" (to make allowances for other forms of consecrated life), and the 1996 Apostolic exhortation *Vita Consecrata*, drawn from the synodal propositions, presents three aspects of religious life or consecrated life — consecration, communion, and mission — by which the life is to be viewed. The language of *Vita Consecrata* presents three groups — the laity, the clergy, and the consecrated — as participating in the life of the Church.[12]

---

[9]Canon 207.1: "Among the Christian faithful by divine institution there exists in the Church sacred ministers, who are also called clerics in law, and other Christian faithful, who are also called laity."

Canon 207.2: "From both groups there exist Christian faithful who are consecrated to God in their own sacred manner and serve the salvific mission of the Church through the profession of the evangelical counsels by means of vows or other sacred bonds recognized and sanctioned by the Church. Such persons also are of service to the saving mission of the Church; although their state does not belong to the hierarchical structure of the Church, they nevertheless do belong to its life and holiness."

[10]John Paul II, "Women's Role in the Church," 35.

[11]The title of the Curial body responsible for religious and consecrated life is the Congregation for Institutes of Consecrated Life and Societies of Apostolic Life, which could indicate a distinction between religious life and other forms of consecrated life. In common usage, including by this very Congregation, "institutes of consecrated life" often applies to religious institutes only. Cf. Congregation for Institutes of Consecrated Life and for Societies of Apostolic Life, Instruction on "Inter-Institute Collaboration for Formation," December 8, 1998.

[12]David N. Power, "Theologies of Religious Life and Priesthood," in *A Concert of Charisms: Ordained Ministry in Religious Life*, ed. Paul K. Hennessey, C.F.C. (Mahwah, N.J.: Paulist Press, 1997), 61–103, 66, citing John Paul II, Apostolic exhortation *Vita Consecrata*,

Naming distinctions among laity, clergy, and consecrated persons can create confusion, and some degree of separatism. In one mode, separating clergy and religious (consecrated persons) from "the laity" creates an apparent equation between the clergy and the religious state (consecrated life), which in effect creates an apparent equation between male dedication to the Church (predominantly as clerics) and female dedication to the Church (as the predominant membership in religious institutes and institutes of consecrated life).[13] This apparent equation is based on perception, not on reality. In actual practice, religious (most often women) and clerics (that is, unmarried clerics) often ally themselves with each other and consider themselves in a separate category from the laity in general and, often, from married deacons. That is, there is an unofficial line of demarcation between those dedicated to the Church as celibates (as religious or clerics) and seculars dedicated to the Church (even married clerics).

Women do not have an avenue for two-sided commitment.

To be clear, the possibilities for men in the Church (as delineated by Canon Law and the Councils) include secular or religious service as bishop, priest, or deacon, or lay person,[14] including specific functions to which only men (religious or lay) may be "installed." That is, while in necessity any lay person may perform the functions of lector or acolyte, only secular or religious men, but not women, may be installed as lectors or acolytes. Secular men may be ordained to the diaconate after marriage,[15] and widowed deacons may not remarry, although some have gained exception to

Origins 25, no. 41 (1996): 681–719 (*Vita Consecrata,* no. 31, "lay faithful," "ordained ministers," and "consecrated persons").

[13] Approximately 72.5 percent of members of religious and secular institutes are female. Most male members of religious and secular institutes are clergy — deacons, priests, or bishops.

[14] That is, service to the Church as either a secular priest or deacon — most often a diocesan priest or deacon — or as a priest, deacon, or laic (brother) within a religious order or institute. Again, "lay" or "laic" in apposition to "clergy" or "cleric" is not the equivalent of "the laity."

[15] Canons 1031.2 and 1042.1. Married men may also be ordained to priesthood after dispensation by the Apostolic See, as in the cases cited earlier regarding married former Episcopal priests (Canon 1047.2.3).

that discipline.[16] There are no restrictions as to marriage for secular men installed as lectors or acolytes, although those most usually installed are already in the seminary career path and expected to promise celibacy before ordination to the transitional diaconate.

The possibilities for women (as delineated in Latin Canon Law and by the Councils) include status as a secular lay person or laic (a lay woman and a member of "the laity") or as a religious lay person or laic (a laywoman and a member of a religious order or institute). The distinctions between clergy and lay persons of import here involve all women, whether members of institutes of consecrated life or not, because the present discussion centers on the inclusion of women (religious or secular) in the clerical state.

The ability to perform some of the functions of clergy, even of those clergy historically in minor orders, have been denied women in modern times. For example, while Canon Law provides that all lay persons may serve as lectors and acolytes, certain of the functions of acolytes were until recently routinely denied women where they involved altar service, despite Canons that expressly pointed to the contrary. Some conservative bishops still maintain older interpretations of Canon and liturgical law.

While the Church today protects women in marriage, and attempts to ensure that a two-sided commitment is permanent, it restricts the possibility of such a covenant with the Church. The primary model for women's permanent commitment to Christ through his Church is profession in an institute of consecrated life. While there are variations, including commitments made in secular institutes or societies of apostolic life (often confused with the active or "apostolic" religious orders or institutes), women most commonly live vowed communal life in religious orders or institutes, having professed solemn or, more ordinarily, simple vows according to the norms of their group's constitutions.

That religious profession is the only method of women's public commitment to the Church in service can lead to misuse, or at

---

[16]Canons 194.1, 3 and 1394.1. I am not aware of any exception for widowed priests' remarriage.

least misunderstanding, of the concept of vows within community, especially if one recognizes self-sufficient monastic communities as the earliest models of religious life. Vowed religious commit to poverty, chastity, and obedience through a specific religious order or institute. While certain religious institutes serve primarily within specific dioceses, members are not vowed in obedience to the diocesan bishop. Yet, as the only method of permanent commitment widely available to women, vowed religious life can be misused and misunderstood both by its members and by Church authority. Specifically, women who might otherwise be secular clerics may choose religious life as a way to permanently serve the Church. Equally, bishops who might otherwise employ women deacons call forth the members of religious institutes to support the diocesan structure. In fact, *Vita Consecrata* comments especially on the particular relationship between diocesan bishops and institutes of diocesan right, asking that they be given "a place in the pastoral plans of the Diocese."[17]

Where women religious venture to serve outside the diocesan or institute structure, ecclesial administrative authorities have the right to terminate the permanent commitments in poverty, chastity, and obedience established among women, because all such bonds are ratified by the Church. In fact, until the 1917 Code of Canon Law diocesan bishops had the right to admit women to diocesan congregations. This former right of the diocesan bishop is perhaps best viewed as a vestige of their ability to call and ordain women deacons to their service.[18]

Particular cases in recent years in the United States may have been justified juridically, but the publicity that surrounded them created the impression that no woman's commitment would be

---

[17] *Vita Consecrata,* no. 48.

[18] "The Constitution '*Conditae,*' December 8, 1900 (sic), giving to the bishop of the diocese the right to admit candidates to the novitiate in diocesan congregations, is modified by Canon 543." Stanislaus Woywod, *A Practical Commentary on the Code of Canon Law,* rev. by Callistus Smith (New York: Joseph F. Wagner, 1957), 247. See Leo XIII, *Constitutio Apostolica de Religiosorum Institutis Vota Simplicia Profitentium "Conditae"* (December 6, 1900).

accepted on a permanent basis as a two-sided one, and that a woman religious superior was not the holder of juridical office.[19]

No doubt men have been dismissed from orders, refused faculties, and put out of religious houses. Such dismissal, refusal, and expulsion continues to this day, yet religious clerics so treated can validly (if illegitimately) claim some permanence to their status as clergy so long as they are not laicized (voluntarily or involuntarily). The public perception, despite Canon Law's contravening provisions, is that for women there is no recourse. Because a woman can only commit herself via a religious order or institute, and because there is no permanent status through which she can be incorporated into the Hierarchy, the impression exists that an "outside agency," specifically, the Congregation for Institutes of Consecrated Life and Societies of Apostolic Life, can and will interfere within women's religious orders.[20] While clerics similarly expelled can be involuntarily laicized, validly received ordination never becomes invalid.[21] The rich tapestry of religious life in the Church is damaged when women religious are treated as clerics, either legally, through forced resignations, or by employment,

---

[19]See especially the case of Agnes Mary Mansour, who for thirty years had been a Sister of Mercy of the Union when in 1983, with the permission of Detroit's Archbishop Edmund Szoka, she became director of the Michigan Department of Social Services, which administered Medicaid funding for abortions. She requested a dispensation from her vows when a papal delegate, then-Auxiliary Bishop Anthony J. Bevilacqua of Brooklyn, informed her she must either resign her position or leave her community. She was not allowed a leave of absence. Had she not resigned her vows, the Sisters of Mercy could have been required to expel her. (Bishop Bevilacqua was soon named Bishop of Pittsburgh, and, later, Archbishop of Philadelphia, and a Cardinal.) An appeal to the Vatican arguing lack of due process by Sisters of Mercy president Sister Teresa Kane (who had appealed to the Pope for the ordination of women in 1979) was denied. At issue: "Mansour has said she personally opposes abortion but that as long as abortion is legal it would be unfair to deny state funding to those women who cannot afford it." David E. Anderson, United Press International, May 25, 1983.

Another case was unrelated to abortion. When asked about the demand that she resign her vows before running for office, Sister of Mercy Arlene Violet, who ran for state attorney general in Rhode Island, said: "It's important to be a Sister of Mercy in reality even if you may have to forfeit being one in name." *New York Times,* January 20, 1984, B-1.

[20]It is not necessary to discuss here status as a diocesan hermit (Canon 603) or status within a secular institute, which are within the purview of the Congregation for Institutes of Consecrated Life and Societies of Apostolic Life. The Congregation for Bishops has competence over personal prelatures.

[21]Canon 290.

where they fill diaconal positions (particularly within the diocesan structure) without benefit of orders.

Religious life as such, especially for women, is not clerical and should not be so perceived. Having said that, however, it must be recognized that beyond baptism there is no permanent sacramental bond for ministry possible between a woman and the Church. The Church has both the right and the need to expect such a permanent sacramental bond.

Permanent commitment should imply permanent relationship.

The perils of a one-sided relationship quickly curb the fire within the hearts of American women who would publicly and permanently follow Christ through the Church. Church authority is essentially unable to permanently incorporate women into the diocesan structure, even given the possibility of conferral of an office for an indeterminate amount of time, and no matter the various Canons that provide for proper remuneration for those who permanently or temporarily dedicate themselves to service of the Church.[22] Any level of permanence or "tenure" does not permanently incorporate an individual into the hierarchical ministerial service of the Church. That permanent incorporation is by entrance into the clerical state.

The present means of entering the clerical state is by ordination to the diaconate.[23] Realistically speaking, since women cannot be ordained to the diaconate, they cannot enter the clerical state. Therefore, there is no permanent hierarchical state any woman may enter. Beyond, there are no provisions for permanent "employment" or support of women through the diocesan structure. Hence, membership in a religious institute or order of women is the only means by which a woman may effectively gain per-

---

[22]Canons 230, 231.

[23]Canon 266.1. "A person becomes a cleric through the reception of the diaconate and is incardinated into the particular Church or personal prelature for whose service he has been advanced" ("Per receptum diaconatum aliquis fit clericus . . ."). Professed members of religious or secular institutes are similarly incardinated (Canons 266.2 and 266.3).

manency in her commitment to serve Christ's people, but that permanent commitment does not relate to ecclesial service in direct line with the bishop. Where they serve the diocesan structure, even as pastoral administrators, women religious, much as secular laity, are mere employees of diocesan structures, without any claim to permanent ecclesial status such as is gained through ordination.[24]

Impermanence in ecclesial service outside the works of a given institute of women religious is but one contemporary difficulty in religious life. Extensive documentation of the drop in the numbers of women religious in the United States merely points to a symptom. In the history of the Church in America, there have been significant contributions by diocesan institutes of women religious, which then initiate service to the Catholic community in ways of their own accord in response to the expressed needs of the diocesan bishop, usually in diocesan structures or works. The local bishop may have apparently been gaining women in his service through the erection of such institutes, but he in no way created a category of women in direct service to the local Church. Consequently, either individual or group discernment preferring less traditional methods of service to the Church on the part of these diocesan institutes of women religious has weakened the underpinnings of some of the parochial or diocesan structures, which depended in large part on the labor of these same women. Yet women who neither control structures nor have a guaranteed place within them are increasingly hesitant to commit their lives to the service of such structures. This fact has become particularly apparent since the close of Vatican II.[25]

Concurrently, in the United States, a number of diocesan com-

---

[24]Canon Law and other Instructions on the permanent diaconate note that neither do permanent deacons have any right to remuneration or support (Canon 281.3). As clerics, deacons are canonically members of the bishop's household and in some, but not all U.S. dioceses, have a claim at least to personal purchase of health and life insurance through the diocesan group plan.

[25]Alice I. Liftin, "Structural Change in U.S. Catholic Women's Orders after 1967: Placing Religious Innovation in Sociological Context" (Ph.D. Diss., Columbia University, 1985).

munities of women have found that ministry in parish schools is only part of what they could be doing. As women, particularly women religious, work in direct service of the parish, as coordinators of religious education or as pastoral ministers, they are performing diaconal service. However, despite canonical possibilities and papal suggestions, women are not working in many other ministries to which they might be appointed, and are rarely ceremonially present in the sanctuary during the celebration of Eucharist.[26]

Often the parish work of women is haphazardly organized and dependent upon individual arrangements with individual pastors. Further, there is no general standard for the focus and content of the programs, although in given dioceses individual bishops are beginning to take more responsibility for ways in which lay ministers are formed, trained, and employed. In the United States, about half of the 281 lay ministry programs are sponsored by a Catholic institution of higher learning (university, college, or seminary) and about half by an archdiocese or diocese. There are a few independent programs. The majority of participants in the programs are women: 60 percent in the academic-based programs and 64 percent in the diocesan and independent programs. More than half the participants (male and female) are between the ages of forty and sixty.[27]

While many are involved in training for ministry in Catholic-sponsored programs, more are enrolled in non-Catholic academic seminaries in preparation for Catholic ministry.[28] Given the large number of persons involved, it would seem appropriate for dioceses to become more formally involved with those training for ministry, both under and not under Catholic auspices. Literally

---

[26]The gradual restrictions relative to women's attendance at the altar came early in the Church. It must be realistically understood, however, that the altar rail symbolically and really separated women from the sacrifice of the altar.

[27]CARA *Catholic Ministry Formation Directory, 1998–1999* (Washington, D.C.: Center for Applied Research in the Apostolate, Georgetown University, 1999).

[28]For example, at Union Theological Seminary in New York, 15 percent of the 300 students identify themselves as Catholic; in any given year nearly half of these are preparing for ministry.

thousands of women are preparing to serve the Church in various ministerial roles.[29]

There is both hierarchical and nonhierarchical ratification of ministry by women.

The singular evolution of the role of spiritual director, an ancient ministry of the Church, has grown increasingly popular in the years since Vatican II. Not surprisingly, women are drawn to this ministry, both as directors and as those whom they accompany. The self-ratification of spiritual directors by the creation of training programs and professional societies, which encourage professional standards of preparation and practice and which seem to serve as an alternative to ordination for Roman Catholic women, deserves close attention as Rome moves toward or away from the ordination of women in general and the diaconate in particular.

The need for training and for the ratification of professional society membership, whether by spiritual directors or by any of a number of other specific ministries within the Church (e.g., hospital chaplaincy and campus ministry), might not be obviated by a return to the female diaconate. However, the client population of training programs and the membership of professional societies might become more balanced according to gender if more women — particularly Roman Catholic women — are welcomed to orders.[30] Professional society membership would no longer be the sole method by which Roman Catholic women could attain professional status.

Besides the nonhierarchical self-ratification of various min-

---

[29]In 1997–98 there were 29,137 persons training for lay ministry in the United States according to the Center for Applied Research in the Apostolate, *The CARA Report* 4, no. 4 (Spring 1999): 14. In contrast, there were 105,870 candidates for priesthood in philosophates and theologates worldwide according to the *Statistical Yearbook of the Church, 1998* (Vatican City: Typis Polyglottis Vaticanis, 1998), 228.

[30]Spiritual Directors International's first conference in San Francisco in 1990 attracted 90 persons; the organization now has 3,063 members in thirty-six countries, over two-thirds female, including in excess of 839 Roman Catholic women religious. It describes itself as "an ecumenical network, [which] fosters the ministry of spiritual direction and on-going development of spiritual directors — women and men, lay and ordained — in the Christian community." See http://www.sdiworld.org.

istries, there are numerous ways by which there have been hierarchical recognitions of ministry by women. Official relationships between women's religious institutes and diocesan bishops are as variegated as the individual institutes and bishops. Often, however, bishops most in need of clergy find that women — both religious and secular — might be better trained and more dedicated than diocesan deacons. Bereft of priests, these bishops have often been able to call upon the larger community of lay men and women, secular and religious, to minister to its own. But there are no guarantees. In many locales (unless the people actually object) the priest or deacon on the horizon signals replacement of the nonordained minister in whatever capacity she — or he — has served.

Concurrently, the obedience of women in service to the local Church is not the same as the obedience of priests and deacons. Secular women make no vows or promises to the bishop. Women who are vowed are most commonly members of religious orders or institutes, whose vows are to and through their own structures, and generally a bishop has only negative authority over them. Because of this, the bishop cannot directly depend upon any woman in the permanent service of the local Church. Any small exceptions only point to the need and possibility for wider opportunity for permanent commitment.

Women must be more formally integrated into public ministry.

Church authority has increasingly and perhaps necessarily developed an administrative Church that exists as a bureaucracy. The Church's bureaucracy creates a self-propelling argument for its own existence, divorced from the integrated service of women. This is not specific to the Church, but is symptomatic of bureaucracy, which always seeks to replicate itself.

But ministry is not bureaucracy. The argument can be made that by nature women are more attuned to the ancient role of deacon than men, and that priesthood has developed into a symbolically male ministry, expressing the concept of Christ as the bridegroom of the Church.[31] This could be true even granting that the well-integrated personality holds both feminine and masculine characteristics. In this construct, the service of deacon might be seen as expressly female, insofar as it is one of complementing and supporting the roles of priests and bishops ordained to service of the Church.

However, permanent deacons are equally "other Christs" in the service of the Church.[32] The emphasis on service within the theology of the diaconate underscores this point even more. The works of service in which permanent deacons are routinely involved are those that are and have been traditionally available to women, that is, works that do not require priestly ordination for their conduct. The restoration of the permanent diaconate has created a class of ordained ministers whose training and formation approaches that of the majority of women working in the Church who, when they find full-time employment in the Church, are working in roles women can and have fulfilled. The distinction is that members of this class of ordained ministers — deacons — have their roles symbolically recognized during liturgical celebrations, and their ministry is equivalently provided for by law. By rescript — a specially requested permission — women can fulfill all the sacramental functions of deacon. Except in mission territories, such rescripts are rare.[33]

A theology of orders that insists that the diaconate is only a step on the way to priesthood (despite the fact that the diaconate is fully incorporated in priesthood) belittles the ministerial function of both the deacon and the priest. The principal objection

---

[31]Matthew 9:15–16; Mark 2:19–21; Luke 5:35–36; John 3:29. Jesus uses the marriage metaphor that the Old Testament uses to express the relationship between God and Israel. Exegetes of this metaphor also point to Ephesians 5:22–31 and 2 Corinthinans 11:2. See, for example, John Paul II, Apostolic exhortation *Pastor dabo vobis*.

[32]"Deacons, too, who are ministers of the mysteries of Jesus ... are not mere servants with food and drink, but emissaries of God's Church.... Similarly, all should respect the deacons as Jesus Christ." Ignatius of Antioch, Letter to the Trallians. *The Liturgy of the Hours*, IV (New York: Catholic Book Publishing Co., 1975), 350, citing Funk, 1, 203–9.

[33]Canon 59.1: "A rescript is an administrative act issued in writing by competent executive authority by which through its very nature a privilege, dispensation, or other favor is granted in response to someone's request." Diocesan bishops in this case would request permission from Rome via their Apostolic Nunciature.

to including women in the diaconate at present seems to center on this fear: that women deacons might be a perceived or real step on the way toward women priests. Leaving that aside, especially as Rome has so ordered, the case for female deacons is still compelling. They who will declare or insist that women cannot be ordained to diaconal service simply declare and insist that women cannot serve the Church and be *directly* both juridically and sacramentally bound to it. Therefore, the Church must formalize the ministry of women.

Summary

The discussion that follows is aimed at supporting the needs of the Church, needs that are not fully served in part because inherent systemic difficulties send mixed signals to the whole Church. An argument for women's ordained ministry addresses the needs of the Church, especially since the Church's categories create a separatism. In fact, women have no avenue for two-sided commitment. Without doubt, permanent commitment should imply permanent relationship. The fact of both hierarchical and nonhierarchical ratification of ministry by women indicates that women must be formally integrated into public ministry. Hence, the Church must formalize the ministry of women.

PART TWO

THE ARGUMENT

The restoration of the female diaconate is necessary
for the continuance of the apostolic life and ministry
of the Roman Catholic Church.

This claim is strong, and intentionally so. The Church at large has suffered its own discontinuance of the tradition of ordained ministry by women for too long, and for its own health truly must restore the traditional role that women for so many centuries had, and still have, now solely in an unordained status. The Church can at present best formalize the ministry of women through the restoration of the female diaconate.

I. Men and women are ontologically equal.

Ecclesiology should better reflect a single-nature anthropology.

The challenge to the Church of the coming century is to build an ecclesiology that is in harmony with its anthropology, that sees women as equally human to men, as persons made in the image and likeness of a God whose infinitude is as it implies and is not limited by sex.[34] This ecclesiology will ultimately be rooted in a single-nature anthropology, which sees human nature and existence as the same for both males and females,[35] and which is reflected in multiple Church documents. As Pope John Paul II has pointed out, the understanding of the essential equality of men and women is rooted in Genesis, and

> To say that man is created in the image and likeness of God means that man is called to exist "for" others, to become a gift.
> This applies to every human being, whether woman or man....[36]

According to John Paul II, factual equality, "asserted from the first page of the Bible in the stupendous narrative of creation," must be reflected in a "culture of equality." The Pope has called for a "culture of equality" that will address "situations in which women live, *de facto* if not legally, in a condition of inferiority."[37] Women, especially Western women in the recent past, are inter-

---

[34] While Canon 208 states that "in virtue of their rebirth in Christ there exists among all the Christian faithful a true equality with regard to dignity and the activity whereby all cooperate in the building up of the Body of Christ in accord with each one's condition and function," it is still possible to infer that "one's condition" of female gender limits "a true equality."

[35] This division is discussed thoroughly in Mary Aquin O'Neill, "Toward a Renewed Anthropology," *Theological Studies* 36 (1975): 734–36, and referred to in the report "Women in Church and Society," Catholic Theological Society of America, 1978, 32.

[36] John Paul II, Apostolic letter *Mulieris Dignitatem*, no. 7. A note refers to "the Fathers of the Church who affirm the fundamental equality of man and woman before God; cf. Origen, *In Jesu nave* IX, 9: PG 12, 878; Clement of Alexandria, *Paed.* 1,4: S. Ch. 70, 128–31; St. Augustine, *Sermo* 51, II, 3: PL 38, 334–35."

[37] John Paul II, "Culture of Equality Is Urgently Needed Today" (June 25, 1995), 1, in *Pope John Paul on the Genius of Women* (Washington, D.C.: United States Catholic Conference, 1997, 1999), 22.

nalizing this recommendation of the Pope, and are recognizing themselves as persons created as equal by a God whose relationship with us is so all-encompassing as to be indescribable, except analogically and with the imperfections of sexual analogy.[38] This metaphor in and of itself creates a tangled problem in a discussion that is at once philosophical, theological, psychological, and literary.

The difficulty in the development of ecclesiology (which is not a matter of changes in history, human emancipatory movements, or even human rights) is that it reflects the requirements of a theological perspective revealed in scripture and explained through the centuries by the Church in its protection of the deposit of faith. So development is sometimes misconstrued as departure. But developed ecclesiology that reflects ontological understandings is not departure, and it does not proceed from the notion that there is any fracture in the realm of being. Rather, as reflected in the papal statements noted above, and in many other documents, such developed ecclesiology reflects the recognition of fracture in the *understanding* of the realm of being, a fracture brought about by misunderstanding and misinterpretations of scripture. Current papal teaching moves toward healing that fracture.

While interpretations of Thomistic systematic theology can argue both that women are and are not ontologically equal to men, the latter interpretation often reduces to physicality. That is, the concept of "nature" can be seen as physical. But interpretations that reduce ontological understandings to mere physicality, and reject any concept of equality between men and women, are false. As Pope John Paul II has written in the encyclical *Evangelium Vitae:*

---

[38]Women have investigated and argued their equal status in many disciplines and multiple fora. The reduction of the discussion is in a simple sentence in Elizabeth A. Johnson's *Friends of God and Prophets; A Feminist Theological Reading of the Communion of Saints* (New York: Continuum, 1998), 227: "Similarly, women friends of God and prophets in the communion of saints today can simply declare of themselves, 'This is what Christ looks like,' affirming in this way their deepest affiliation and resisting its denial until the heart of officialdom is converted."

In transforming culture so that it supports life, women occupy
a place, in thought and action, which is unique and deci-
sive. It depends on them to promote a "new feminism" which
rejects the temptation of imitating models of "male domina-
tion," in order to acknowledge and affirm the true genius of
women in every aspect of the life of society, and overcome all
discrimination, violence, and exploitation.[39]

The Church, which is fundamentally a communion of the baptized, can and must better reflect a single-nature anthropology.
All in the Church are, by right and force of baptism, equal. It is of
course right, proper, and necessary to draw distinctions. However,
some distinctions made in arguments against including women in
ordained ministry support discrimination, violence, and exploitation within the context of Church. These distinctions are not
drawn from Gospel values or from scripture, but rather have accrued through acceptance of the very culture the Gospel stands
in opposition to. That a contemporary understanding of ontology would support rejection of the accretions of another age is
fundamentally reasonable; that the Church would for any reason
fear acceptance of contemporary understandings of ontology in
relation to its fundamental teachings is not.

The "iconic argument" attacks single-nature anthropology.

A principal argument against the ordination of women to priesthood is known as the "iconic argument." Over the centuries the
Church has developed a theological language that calls Christ the
"spouse" of the Church, which is often referred to as "she." Church
teaching dictates that only men, specifically ordained male priests
(and bishops), can represent Christ and act *in persona Christi*
(*in persona Christi capitis ecclesiae*) in this analogous relationship.
Such a construct bespeaks the dual-nature anthropology discussed
above, in which each sex has different and distinct roles beyond

---

[39]John Paul II, Encyclical *Evangelium Vitae*, no. 99 (March 25, 1995), in *Pope John Paul II on the Genius of Women*, 73.

the biological, yet stemming from the biological. It is a two-nature vision of humanity. That is, either the human has one nature and two genders, and therefore is equal if not the same, or the human has two natures, neither equal nor the same. It is important to recognize that some theological language bespeaks a dual-nature anthropology and considers men and women neither equal nor the same.

The way in which such a concept is received is that men and women are not equal *because* they are not the same, and "sameness" is determined by gender, not by nature.

Therefore, many persons are rightly insulted by the iconic argument, which is explained by Avery Dulles thusly:

> To dispel any remaining doubts, it may be important to show some intrinsic grounds why women are unsuitable for priestly ministry. In *Ordinatio Sacerdotalis* the Pope relies only on arguments from authority, but mentions in passing that there are "theological reasons which illustrate the appropriateness of the divine provision." In *Mulieris Dignitatem* (1988) he used the so-called "iconic" argument, to the effect that the priest at the altar acts in the person of Christ the Bridegroom. These theological reasons, while not strictly probative, show why it was fitting for Christ to have decided freely to reserve priestly service to men. If the maleness of the priest is essential to enable him to act symbolically *in persona Christi* in the eucharistic sacrifice, it follows that women should not be priests. The "iconic" argument is complex and difficult to handle, but it does in the end give intelligibility to the authoritative teaching.[40]

Note that the iconic argument as delineated here does not represent that women cannot be ordained, only that women cannot perform priestly ministry. Further, the iconic argument is applicable only to the priesthood. Dulles writes that "in *Mulieris Dignitatem* (1988) [John Paul II] used the so-called 'iconic' argument, to the effect that the priest at the altar acts in the

---

[40] Avery Dulles, "Women's Ordination and Infallibility, 2: Tradition Says No," *The Tablet*, December 9, 1995, 1573. John Paul II's Apostolic letter *Ordinatio Sacerdotalis* (1994) is the most recent papal statement on admission of women to ministerial priesthood.

person of Christ the Bridegroom."[41] Therefore, Christ, bridegroom
of the Church, can be effectively represented only by a male
person.[42]

This view is independent of the shift in contemporary theology
to a focus on the priest as minister, who by and because of his
ministry presides at the altar. The iconic argument as presented
here seems to reduce the priest to confector of Eucharist, exclusive of any pastoral relationship with or charge of the community.
Christ's act in choosing apostles, the basic constitutive element
of the Church, is authoritative, but it is impossible to impute that
Christ chose only men because he believed only men could represent the fullness of his humanity. We know only that Christ
chose men.

Even so, there is an ecclesial acceptance of an all-male priesthood that supports both the "arguments from authority" Dulles
refers to and the iconic argument, which recognizes the priest as
icon of Christ. One might agree that the cultural appurtenances
of contemporary priesthood are such as to make entrance into
it iconically impossible for women. However, this second impossibility is not because of the intrinsic nature of priesthood, but
due to the Church's cultural understanding of priesthood. That
is, the present ecclesial acceptance of the iconic argument is at
its root a cultural one. It is not that the priest must be the icon
of Christ, but that the priest-candidate must be the icon of the
Church's understanding of priest. The Church at large has therefore accepted an iconic argument because of its understanding of

---

[41]"It is the Eucharist above all that expresses the redemptive act of Christ the Bridegroom toward the Church the Bride. This is clear and unambiguous when the sacramental
ministry of the Eucharist, in which the priest acts 'in persona Christi,' is performed by a
man. This explanation confirms the prohibition of the Declaration *Inter Insigniores*, published at the behest of Paul VI in response to the question concerning the admission of
women to the ministerial priesthood." See John Paul II, Apostolic letter *Mulieris Dignitatem*,
no. 25.

[42]Note that *Mulieris Dignitatem* states "as members of the Church, men too are included in the concept of 'bride,'" leaving the inevitable question as to who can be included
in the concept of bridegroom, but supporting the notion that both men and women, as
bride-Church, can be symbolically represented by male and female deacons. See John
Paul II, Apostolic letter *Mulieris Dignitatem*, no. 25.

a priesthood that excludes women not so much theologically as culturally ("iconically"), and that cultural ("iconic") understanding and acceptance supports exclusion of any further theological reflection on the matter.

However, whether or not the iconic argument holds, it is irrelevant to this discussion. It may in fact support the notion of ordained women deacons. The matter at hand is not whether women may serve as priests, but whether women may be ordained deacons. That Church authority at this point has commanded an end to argument on behalf of priesthood for women sets in *bas relief* the lack of argument against restoration of the female diaconate.

The dichotomous relationships between men and women in the Church have in their reflection implications relative to the understanding of the nature of women and the possibilities for women to act in the name of Christ juridically and sacramentally. Hence, we leave aside considerations regarding priesthood, and therefore relative to the ability of women to act *in persona Christi* as understood through the cultural basis of the iconic argument, and focus rather on the diaconate, which is supported by correct understanding of single-nature anthropology and would include women's acting *in nomine Christi* (*in nomine ecclesiae Christi*).

Single-nature anthropology argues for equality.

The essential understandings relative to the equality of men and women as concerns the ministry of service are based in anthropology. The question of dual- or single-nature anthropology has important ramifications, especially in light of some feminist arguments. Dual-nature anthropology presents women as typified by a view of Mary, the Mother of Jesus, in complete surrender to God in a passivity that is almost quietist. This limitation of Mary's supreme "fiat!" is inextricably bound to a cultural concept of "feminine nature," which by extension describes and prescribes the relationship of all women to all men and women and, thus, of all women to the Church. This view can also call woman incapable of doing anything else in relation to anyone or anything else but surrender, and reduces her from the totally human in the face of God (if one subscribes to single-nature anthropology) to someone or something less than that. Obviously it does not recognize the *action* of surrender, either of Mary or of her Son on the Cross.

The notion of the woman as both embodiment and ensoulment of the passive, which has been called the idea of the "feminine soul," is the most serious myth to be overcome. This approach to a dual-nature anthropology, the argument for a "feminine soul," has been used to oppress women in their interiorizing the powerlessness of Jesus as sacrificial victim to the point where any exercise of power or authority is seen as "unfeminine," often by men *and* women. Concurrent with this understanding is the argument that the surrender of Jesus in powerlessness to the Cross was supreme passivity, not supreme activity. Yet the ultimate act of "power" is precisely such a surrender into "son-ship" and can be made only by an adult human secure in both faith and personality. (The concept of misunderstood powerlessness pushed from another direction finds any exercise of power ultimately un-Christian. It is a mistaken notion that cheapens both the concepts of leadership and of pacifism.)

Acceptance by women of the dual-nature anthropology, this "feminine soul," arguably would allow, and in many cases has allowed, men to seek and gain control of women's ideas about themselves, rendering women powerless to direct their own lives. Having convinced women of their innate passivity to the point that attempts to develop other areas of their personalities were criticized as specifically unfeminine, these same men reign powerful over women in a controlling and ultimately stifling way. Women denied freedom are not free souls; their growth is stunted and distorted.

Mary Daly puts this point most strongly at the beginning of *The Church and the Second Sex:*

> Symbolic idealization tends to dupe women into satisfaction with the narrow role imposed upon them. Made to feel guilty or "unnatural" if they rebel, many have been condemned to

a restricted or mutilated existence in the name of religion. Moreover, the Church has been described as a pressure group exercising influence on the practical level, through whatever press, media and political, religious and social organizations it controls, to prevent changes which would improve the condition of women.[43]

That is, in Daly's view Church structure argues against that which it teaches and desires: the formation of the whole individual who will recognize that he — or she — is made in the image and likeness of God.

A fully-formed spirituality, however, must recognize the relationship between the active and passive (or, perhaps, between active and contemplative), which easily although incorrectly equates with the masculine and feminine principles of our personalities.[44] If the project of our lives is for us to become fully human, then we must go beyond the principles of personality that specifically reflect our gender and yet not argue for androgyny. A dual-nature anthropology argues that men are the embodiment of "activity" and women are the embodiment of "passivity." It does not follow that only men can be "active" and only women can be "contemplative"; characteristics of the soul are not wholly engendered in the body. The subsuming of the entire feminine personality to a kind of passive entropy then echoed by actions or status in the world and, especially in the Church, has its foundation in the arguments against ontological understandings of equality and against single-nature anthropology.

Projection of a dual-nature anthropology limits God and Church.

Theology derived from anthropology, whether male-centered or female-centered, ultimately limits God. One feminist writer, Marilyn Chapin Massey, argues that a "phallocentric religion and male

---

[43]Mary Daly, *The Church and the Second Sex* (Boston: Beacon Press, 1968, 1985), 53.

[44]The mixed metaphor is intentional: prayer is more accurately termed "receptive," a passive activity, or an active passivity. The contemplative life may be more active than the active life, which can be overwhelmingly passive, but that is subject for another discussion.

gods" underlie men's political and social claim to superiority in the world.[45] She is joined by writers who state that such a "phallo-centric religion" and attendant male gods underlie men's political and social claim to superiority in the Church. These writers dismiss Church arguments forbidding ordination of women to priesthood and the episcopacy in concert with arguments that seek to forestall the restoration of the female diaconate. As to combining consid-erations of priesthood and diaconate as matters of power, we must bifurcate the issue even more strongly if the discussion relative to the ordination of women to the diaconate is to progress, for those who hold to the iconic argument as regards priesthood will not allow its content to be dismissed. To be sure, careful writers never exclude women from orders altogether, only from ordination to priesthood, and most current statements that center on the pro-hibition against women being ordained to priesthood seem rooted in the iconic argument, with argumentation that Christ chose only male apostles, and that choice is authoritative and permanently binding.[46]

There is no need here to either prove or disprove the concept of a male God as theological fact or cultural preference. Unfortu-nately, some Christian feminists have argued for the philosophical removal of the concept of a male God in a negative fashion. Rather than develop the philosophical removal of the concept of a male God in a positive fashion, that is, instead of refusing to limit God, they appear to develop a replacement female Goddess who is equally limited and therefore equally inappropriate.[47]

The God of philosophy is neither male nor female; the God of

[45]Marilyn Chapin Massey, *Feminine Soul: The Fate of an Ideal* (Boston: Beacon Press, 1975), 175.

[46]"It might indeed be unjust to exclude a whole class from ordination on grounds that were arbitrary, but not if the very nature of priesthood, as determined by Christ, requires male gender." Dulles, "Women's Ordination and Infallibility," 1573. Dulles never appears to preclude the possibility of women's ordination to the diaconate, only to priesthood.

[47]Goddess feminism has been described and explored by a number of writers, including Carol P. Christ, "Symbols of Goddess and God," in *The Book of the Goddess, Past and Present,* ed. Carl Olson (New York: Crossroad, 1985), 231–51, and Nellie Morton, "Goddess as Metaphoric Image," in her *The Journey Is Home* (Boston: Beacon, 1985), 147–75, and more recently by Carol P. Christ, *Rebirth of the Goddess: Finding Meaning in Feminist Spirituality* (Reading, Mass.: Addison-Wesley, 1997).

theology is both. The improper projection of man's essence can reduce his understanding of God to another male in the mirror, and the same is true of women. Some Goddess-centered feminists may reject the rest of the world, and especially the Church, as a coalition of institutions built by men reflecting and supporting men's mirrored God. But mimetic reality for these women often absolutely rejects the solutions of men, and suggests that *no* institution — or notion of God — is properly "human" unless it is wholly feminine. Goddess-centered feminists do what they accuse men of doing, in the reverse. Hence, a dual-nature anthropology, whether male or female, improperly limits God and, by extension, the Church.

The rejection of single-nature anthropology results in division according to gender.

As a result of such dual-nature anthropology, Goddess-centered feminists reject the order of grace in the Church as it has been understood and described in an arguably patriarchal fashion, because they see in its patriarchal fashioning the reflection of masculine projections of human nature. The mistake they make is to reject it in favor of one fashioned matriarchically because of feminine projections of human nature. The more appropriate view allows for complementarity of gender without arguing for superiority.

With some feminists' rejection of patriarchal structures and patriarchal rituals comes an increase in the assertion of feminine structures and feminine rituals, especially in the United States, where the economic and legal stringencies that once refused women the opportunity to choose among or between views of themselves are increasingly loosening. In fact, where such stringencies remain, either in the Church or in the secular society as a whole, they are attacked as politically, rather than personally, binding. Beyond, because of the pervasive nature of U.S. media and media products, the "feminist" attitude, for good or for ill, is a worldwide phenomenon even in underdeveloped nations, where it will grow faster because initial technological inroads into those cultures will far outstrip the present technological infrastructures of developed nations. Because of the rapid incursion of advanced telecommunications into multiple levels of disparate societies, what was once an American phenomenon is now a worldwide one, and growing. Hence, women worldwide are seeking more, and more appropriate, recognition of the uses of their time and talents.

When women do not advance within structures, it is commonly argued that they have been eliminated politically because of their sex, and this is often quite true. Much has been written on this. The conundrum becomes: how can a woman advance in a male structure and maintain her feminine self? The knot is cut once "feminine" is redefined.

The writer Virginia Woolf once advised that a woman needs both economic independence and "a room of one's own" in which to live a creative intellectual and, it must be added, spiritual life.[48] When Woolf wrote, the numbers of women who actually could devote their lives to letters or philosophy were appreciably smaller than today. Possibilities for women were once limited by the fact of circumstance within the institutions to which they faithfully belonged. It remains that, worldwide, the increased possibilities for women are still mainly in woman-built and woman-controlled institutions and organizations, despite the tenuous hold women often have on these institutions and organizations. Some women are looking outside to other (coincidentally more powerful) traditionally male-dominated paths to service, but many are recreating women-controlled structures along masculine models, that is, organized hierarchically. The competing "feminine" organization principle is nonhierarchical and more egalitarian (the wheel versus the pyramid), and while it echoes the communal organizational preference of the Church, it undermines the organizational necessities of a juridical structure.

There is ultimate danger in either managerial style: overly "fem-

---

[48]Virginia Woolf, *A Room of One's Own* (New York: Harcourt Brace Jovanovich, 1929, 1957).

inine" (communal) has as a danger unaccountable manipulation of the group; overly "masculine" (juridical) has as a danger bureaucratic stagnation due to fear of acting by lower echelons. Suffice it to say that the balance of nature needs be echoed in the structures of the Church, so communal balances juridical, collegial balances collaborative, ecclesial balances political.

American women have developed many all-women institutions, most of which were originally organized with the typical top-down organizational structure of men's organizations. Hundreds of schools, hospitals, and social service agencies founded, developed, and staffed by women religious in the United States formed the backbone of American healthcare and of Catholic education for the first half of the twentieth century. In recent years, however, women-founded and women-run organizations have been seen as separatist, rather than as complementary. The extreme example of women promoting women in women's institutions that are intentionally separatist is reflected in the kind of "Women-Church" first described by Rosemary Radford Ruether.[49] The development of such parallel structures with concomitant rituals is a reality of the Roman Catholic Church today, primarily in the United States, and increasingly in Western Europe and other highly developed areas of the world.[50] The "Women-Church" described by Ruether is an anti-institutional yet institutionalized expression of the "feminine soul"; it perhaps does not argue strongly enough from a single-nature anthropology that it is the ontological reality of the Incarnation that allows us to under-

---

[49]Rosemary Radford Ruether, *Women-Church: Theology and Practice* (San Francisco: Harper & Row, 1985).

[50]"All-female Eucharist services have been held for years, usually in private homes. But at a time when the Catholic Church has hardened its stance against ordaining women, such services are becoming more public.... Women Church Convergence, a coalition of 35 liberal Catholic groups, has started holding female-led Eucharist services in public places, including a women's shelter and a Protestant church." Caryle Murphy, "Catholic Women Adopt Their Own Eucharistic Rites." See *Washington Post*, July 28, 1998, A10. See "Women's Groups Risk Censure by Holding Own Eucharist," *Dallas Morning News*, September 5, 1998, 62. See also Sheila Durkin Dierks, *Women Eucharist* (Boulder, Colo.: WovenWord Press, 1997); Mary Beben and Bridget Mary Meehan, *Walking the Prophetic Journey* (Boulder, Colo.: WovenWord Press, 1998).

stand ourselves — male and female — as made in the image and
likeness of God.

Christ as exemplar of all humanity presents men and women as ontologically equal.

The philosophical-theological construct of the Christian God is
not the God in a mirror held up to either male or female nature.
The Christian God, who encompasses maleness and femaleness,
whose notion is supported in medieval discussions, is understood
in part through the reflections of both male and female nature.
God become human, whom Christians know as Christ, is exemplar
to women and to men, *precisely* because in his Incarnation he
became *fully* human. That is, God did not become fully male to
the exclusion of becoming fully female; God become "man" *means*
God become "human." To restrict the Incarnation is to restrict
the act of Incarnation. It is the response and the responsibility of
the human — male or female — to draw from within his or her
likeness to Christ, and that likeness begins with humanity as a
whole concept, not with sexuality as a restricting limitation.

Without doubt, we move toward our humanity only in imita-
tion of Christ. As Carolyn Osiek has pointed out, "Our common
human call to transformation in Christ challenges all of us, female
and male, to welcome and cherish within ourselves both sides of
both feminine and masculine characters."[51] This is a psychologi-
cally whole as well as a theologically realistic approach. We can
agree that such a transformation creates the balanced personality that can relate to a Christianity of humanity rather than a
Christianity of patriarchy or a Christianity of matriarchy.

Christian tradition is full of images of God that are specifically
male. On the philosophical level, God the Father is equally limiting, and equally incorrect, to God the Mother. It is possible,
however, that it is equally limiting to reject the Father, the Son,
and the Holy Spirit for the Creator, Redeemer, and Sanctifier, no

---

[51]Carolyn Osiek, *Beyond Anger: On Being a Feminist in the Church* (New York: Paulist
Press, 1986), 62.

matter how true these descriptors are of their action. Accepting the latter formula (Creator, Redeemer, and Sanctifier) as the sole formula eliminates a great deal of very rich tradition and unnecessarily limits the Trinity. The formula Creator, Redeemer, and Sanctifier can also lend itself to confusions in ritual, and eventually to a rejection of the very real and very human male person Christ. Perhaps here the formulation of Richard of St. Victor: *diligens, dilectus, condilectus* (understood as loving one, beloved, and co-beloved) is more appropriate as the way to know and love the Trinity intellectually and wholly, that is, both within and beyond sexuality.[52]

That men and women are ontologically identical, that is, ontologically beyond sexuality in their substance while embracing sexuality in their accidents, argues even more strongly for the all-encompassing nature of God as reflected in Christ's human nature and, ultimately, in the whole body of Christ, the Church, which in and of itself reflects the complementarity that is the fullness of God. Hence, Christ could not ask his Church not to reflect his perfection: it is the Incarnation that argues the ontological equality of men and women.

Summary

Ecclesiology should reflect a single-nature anthropology. The iconic argument attacks a single-nature anthropology, which in and of itself is an argument for equality. The projection of a dual-nature anthropology limits both God and Church. The rejection of single-nature anthropology results in division according to gender. So, Christ as exemplar of all humanity presents men and women as ontologically equal.

---

[52] I reject those implications of creationist spirituality that reject the inherent sexuality of all of nature.

II. The Church has given reasons why women, although ontologically equal to men, may not be ordained to priesthood.

Closing priesthood to women does not preclude the diaconate for women.

Church documents have been relatively consistent in recognizing the ontological equality of women. This recognition, however, does not in and of itself allow for women to receive all sacraments equally. A portion of the reason for this disallowance is both the expansion of the notion and concept of "sign" within sacramental theology, and the lack of clear separation among the three grades of orders.

With priesthood (and therefore with regard to the sacrament of orders as it involves priesthood), the theological notion of "sign" has essentially (and mistakenly) incorporated not only the matter and form of the sacrament, but the matter of the ordinand (the person ordained). In current teaching, priestly ordination, unlike other sacraments, depends not only on how the sacrament is celebrated on behalf of the human person, but also on the sex of the human person receiving the sacrament. That is, priestly ordination is not restricted because women are unable to receive ordination. Rather, priestly ordination is restricted because of priesthood's relation to the sacraments of Eucharist and reconciliation and the teaching that the celebrant of these two sacraments must physically resemble Christ and those men whom it is certainly known he chose as his immediate apostles.

Reformation arguments against the very concept of sacramental ordination stressed a ministerial priesthood drawn from the community, unrelated to the specific institution of a sacrament by Christ. In defense of the doctrine of the sacrament of orders, the Church emphasized the priest's cultic functions — celebration of Eucharist and ability to remit sins — and gave less emphasis to the biblical and patristic heritage of a ministerial priesthood. The cultic function of priest came to be stressed in the iconic argument.

36

Presently, Church authority, in the person of John Paul II and the Congregation for the Doctrine of the Faith, states that the Church does not have the authority to confer priesthood (and episcopacy) upon women.[53] However, ordination to the diaconate does not imply ability to be ordained to the priesthood (hence the revival of the "permanent diaconate"). The diaconate is specifically recognized as a ministry of service separate from (although included in) priesthood. No definitive statement about the power or authority of the Church to confer the diaconate — specifically, diaconal ordination — on women has been made. In fact, a definitive statement on the questions of ordination of women to the diaconate often has been deferred for "further study,"[54] and significant discussion has revolved around whether the deaconesses of the early Church actually received sacred ordination.[55]

The discussion about whether women once received sacred orders has often been tied to whether the office of deaconess was exactly equivalent to the office of deacon. The cultural milieu of the ancient Church would not allow such equality in the modern sense, so it is sufficient to know that there were male and female deacons, or deacons and deaconesses. In fact, the cultural milieu of the ancient Church would *require* both male and female deacons, or deacons and deaconesses. The operative question is not how the Church once met its mission and needs, but rather how it will meet its current mission and needs, recognizing that while the Church has given reasons why women, although onto-

---

[53]Independent, that is, of any consideration of whether the Church has the power to do so.

[54]Sacred Congregation for the Doctrine of the Faith, *Inter Insigniores*, "Declaration on the Question of Admission to the Ministerial Priesthood," October 15, 1976. The diaconate "should be kept for the future and not be touched upon in the present document." "A Commentary on the Declaration," *Origins* 6, no. 33 (February 3, 1977): 524–30, 526. All citations to the document following are from *Origins* 6, no. 33 (February 3, 1977): 517–24. *Inter Insigniores* was published in *Acta Apostolicae Sedis* 69 (1977): 98–116, and in *The Jurist* 37 (Summer–Fall 1977): 325–39.

[55]Women's ordination ceremonies were essentially identical to ceremonies for male deacons. If women deacons did not receive ordination, then neither did male deacons, making the objection moot. See Paul F. Bradshaw, *Ordination Rites of the Ancient Churches of East and West* (New York: Pueblo, 1990).

logically equal to men, may not be ordained to priesthood, closing priesthood to women does not preclude the diaconate for women.

Diaconal orders do not imply priestly orders.

The challenge to the Church, should it recognize a ministerial need for women deacons, is to distinguish orders. That is, the Church needs to more clearly recognize that conferral of ordination to the diaconate does not automatically imply the ability of the ordinand to be ordained priest or bishop. Even if the ability of women to be ordained to the diaconate did imply that women could also be ordained priests and bishops, the Pope has stated he does not have the authority to do so. Therefore, those who argue that reception of diaconal orders by women implies the possibility of the reception of priestly orders by women argue against explicit papal statements. Until this misconception is cleared, the Church will be unable to call forth women deacons.

Sacraments are open to all human persons.[56]

Without digressing into an entire history of sacraments in the Church, it is still well to recall here that the precise definition of "sacrament" was in doubt for a great part of the Church's history. The early Church had numerous sacraments, but in time "sacrament" came to define an act instituted by Christ to give grace to a specific individual. The Church's definitive statements on sacraments issued by the Council of Trent (1545–63) grew from both positive and negative argumentation.

The earlier attempts by Hugh of St. Victor and others in the twelfth century to define "sacrament" more precisely are enlightening. He named several — monastic vows, dedication of a Church, death and judgment — that we do not presently understand as sacraments. Hugh of St. Victor's definition reads thusly:

> Now if any one wishes to define more fully and more perfectly what a sacrament is, he can say: "A sacrament is a corporeal

---

[56]Unless impeded by divine or ecclesiastical law.

or material element set before the senses without, representing by similitude and signifying by institution and containing by sanctification some invisible and spiritual grace." This definition is recognized as so fitting and perfect that it is found to befit every sacrament and a sacrament alone. For every thing that has these three is a sacrament, and every thing that lacks these three cannot be called a sacrament.

For every sacrament ought to have a kind of similitude to the thing itself of which it is the sacrament, according to which it is capable of representing the same thing; every sacrament ought to have also institution through which it is ordered to signify this thing and finally sanctification through which it contains that thing and is efficacious for conferring the same on those to be sanctified.[57]

Note the emphasis on those to be sanctified. The understanding of a sacrament as an act through which grace is received by a person is here reinforced. This understanding had been a fairly constant notion in the development of sacramental theology. The various questions regarding what precisely constituted a sacrament revolved around the manner in which grace might be bestowed and upon whom or what grace might be bestowed. The focus on *only* the human person having the ability to receive grace developed over time.

So in the beginning of the twelfth century, when Peter Lombard in *The Four Books of Sentences* attempts a synthesis of theology and a definition of the number of sacraments, he presents the sacrament as sign and distinguishes Augustine's definitions of seven centuries prior. Peter Lombard does not dispute Augustine's statement: "A sacrament is the visible form of an invisible grace," on the assumption, again, that the sacrament is the act by which the human person receives grace. Peter Lombard writes further:

---

[57]Hugh of St. Victor, *On the Sacraments of the Christian Faith*, I, 9 (1140), trans. Roy J. Deferrari, *Hugh of St. Victor on the Sacraments of the Christian Faith* (Cambridge: Medieval Academy of America, 1951), 155, as quoted in James F. White, *Documents of Christian Worship: Descriptive and Interpretive Sources* (Louisville: Westminster John Knox Press, 1992), 121.

A sacrament bears a likeness of that thing whose sign it is. "For if sacraments did not have a likeness of the things whose sacraments they are, they would properly not be called sacraments" [Augustine]. For that is properly called a sacrament which is a sign of the grace of God and a form of invisible grace, so that it bears its image and exists as its cause. Sacraments were instituted, therefore, for the sake, not only of signifying, but also of sanctifying.[58]

That the sacrament signifies is not to say that the person who receives the sacrament must also signify, although the extensions of the development of the theology of orders has had this accretion over the years, so that the outward sign of the sacrament has been, in the case of orders, transmuted to the outward sign of the person who receives the sacrament. That is, the person who receives the sacrament must also serve as sign of the sacrament, above and beyond the actual sign of the sacrament. Specifically, in this case "sign" seems confused with "symbol."

Church teaching restricts priestly orders because of its understanding of sign and symbol.

The original constitutive elements of the sacrament (the outward sign), "words and things" as Peter Lombard calls them, or, form and matter, seem to have transmuted to include the very human (who will symbolize Christ) receiving the sacrament. That is, the person receiving the sacrament seems included in the matter of the sacrament. The modern declaration of what comprises the matter of the sacrament of orders (the imposition of hands) and what comprises the form of the sacrament of orders (the words determining the meaning of the matter), does not mention gender.[59] However, the sacrament of orders as regards priesthood implicitly

---

[58] Peter Lombard, *The Four Books of the Sentences*, IV Distinction I, 1–2, trans. Owen R. Ott, Library of Christian Classics 10:338–41, as quoted in White, *Documents of Christian Worship*, 122–23.

[59] Pius XII, Apostolic constitution *Sacramentum Ordinis* (1947), in *The Christian Faith in the Doctrinal Documents of the Catholic Church*, ed. J. Neuner and J. Dupuis (Bangalore: Theological Publications in India, 1991), 554.

if not explicitly requires maleness; that is, the sacrament of orders as an outward sign depends on the symbol of the male in
representing Christ.

If this is read to exclude women from *any* sacramental ordination, then the female human is defective matter (for this
sacrament). If the female human is not defective matter, and
women therefore can receive this sacrament as a sign, then the
sacrament of orders may be received equally by men and women.
The sacrament can be received equally because there is no explicit connection between the form and matter of the sacrament
of orders and maleness or femaleness:

> By virtue of our supreme apostolic authority we declare with
> sure knowledge and, as far as it may be necessary, we deter-
> mine and ordain: the matter of the holy orders of diaconate,
> presbyterate and episcopate is the laying on of hands alone,
> and the sole form is the words determining the application of
> the matter, words by which the effects of the sacrament — that
> is, the power of Order and the grace of the Holy Spirit — are
> unequivocally signified and which for this reason are accepted
> and used by the Church.[60]

The question is whether *all* who receive the sacrament of orders must be able to symbolize Christ as Church teaching defines
the manner of symbolizing Christ (i.e., "natural resemblance"). It
would seem that where the Church defines the ordinand as a male
symbol of Christ, a woman may not be ordained to that rank. But,
equally, where the Church defines the ordinand as a minister and
representative of the Church, a woman ought to be able to be
ordained to that rank. Such an understanding would accede to
the current understanding of the Church.

The historical development of sacramental theology would suggest this notion. In defining and numbering the sacraments, Peter
Lombard specifically approached the sacraments of the new law,
the law of Christ which removed all such distinctions. He wrote:

---

[60]Pius XII, Apostolic constitution *Sacramentum Ordinis* (1947), in *Doctrinal Documents
of the Catholic Church,* ed. Neuner and Dupuis, 554.

Now let us approach the sacraments of the new law, which are: baptism, confirmation, the bread of blessing, that is, the eucharist, penance, extreme unction, orders, marriage. Of these, some provide a remedy against sin and confer assisting grace, such as baptism; others are only a remedy, such as marriage; others strengthen us with grace and power, such as the eucharist and orders.[61]

The sacraments of the new law that "strengthen us with grace and power," especially Eucharist and orders, are intriguingly intertwined with the process by which the whole Church is incorporated into the life of Christ. The example of baptism as a sacramental remedy against sin *and* an act that confers assisting grace (as with penance and extreme unction), and that sacrament which is *only* a remedy against sin (matrimony), stand apart from those that strengthen with grace and power, namely, Eucharist and orders (and probably confirmation in this construct). There is no qualification as to who might be strengthened, and no prohibition in any theological construct from anyone receiving a remedy against sin, and so the sign (comprised of matter and form) of the sacrament is that which effects a strengthening with grace and power. That is, the sacrament comprises the strengthening with grace and power, and neither the matter nor the form involves the recipient.[62]

It is the Church that restricts priesthood to men.

The Church's more recently developed theology of orders specifies maleness as implicit to the fact and function of priesthood. It would seem that the specific prohibition relative to the ordination of women to priesthood rests in the argument that the effector of

---

[61]Peter Lombard, *The Four Books of Sentences, IV,* Distinction II, 1, trans. Owen R. Ott, Library of Christian Classics 10:344–45, as quoted in White, *Documents of Christian Worship,* 123.

[62]Peter Lombard names seven grades within orders: "In the sacrament of the sevenfold Spirit there are seven ecclesiastical degrees, namely, doorkeeper [porter], lector, exorcist, acolyte, subdeacon, deacon, priest; all, however, are called clerics, that is, those chosen by lot [Acts 1:26]." Peter Lombard, *The Four Books of Sentences, IV,* Distinction XXIV, 1–3, trans. Owen R. Ott, Library of Christian Classics 10:349, as quoted in White, *Documents of Christian Worship.* 124.

two specific sacraments, Eucharist and reconciliation, must act *in persona Christi*. Further, in order to act *in persona Christi*, the person must naturally resemble Christ (be a "sign" of Christ, here understood as "symbol") in body as well as in spirit. Hence the support of the iconic argument from a root in sacramental theology, in addition to scripture and ecclesiology.

A reasonable person may disagree, arguing that there is nothing implicitly "male" about the function of priest, specifically about the function of priest in reconciliation (an inherently juridical act, as well as one that imparts grace as a remedy) or in Eucharist (a communal act that requires the assembly to be in union with the whole Church). This same reasonable person, however, must note that the social accretions of priesthood, both within and without liturgy, rest on a symbolic understanding of priesthood that includes maleness. There is no such symbolic understanding of the diaconate that includes maleness. So the iconic argument supports only restrictions relative to ordination to priesthood and episcopacy.

That is, the iconic argument as applied to *all* grades of orders rests on the same pedestal from which it falls: that ministry is inherently male (and reflective of the maleness of Christ) is a natural fact of its development and institution by Christ; that ministry is inherently human (and reflective of the humanity of Christ) is equally a natural fact of its development and further institution by the Church. The distinction is that the former serves to restrict ordained priesthood to men, while the latter serves to open the ordained diaconate to women.

The basic argument against the ordination of women to priesthood and episcopacy essentially rests on the iconic argument, as it has received the transferred notion of "sign" from that which is effected to him whom it affects (recognizing the development of the notion that as Christ removed sin and effected Eucharist, so also must the person who imitates Christ in this way resemble him so as to be a "sign" acting *in persona Christi*). In this construct, "symbol" is used to separate that which represents (symbol) from that which points to that which is represented (sign).

So, effectively, while a woman might be able to be ordained a priest, to receive and participate in the "sign" of the sacrament of orders as regards priesthood, she might not be able to fully present herself as "symbol" of priest (or bishop) as priesthood has accrued cultural definition over the life of the Church. This is both the explanation and the conundrum of the iconic argument, which requires a "natural resemblance" to Christ. It is impossible to argue that a woman cannot represent Christ except through the iconic argument, and the iconic argument is only persuasive when considered in the cultural context.

Church authority's response to the calls of the contemporary culture is still "no."

The relatively recent flurry of documents and discussion about the ordination of women to priesthood was apparently most directly inspired by the ordination of women to priesthood within various national Anglican Churches, most notably the ordination of Episcopal women to priesthood in Philadelphia in 1973, and the consequent ecumenical discussions as priesthood increasingly was granted to women by Anglicans. The then-illegal 1973 ordinations were also followed by significant public discussion and comment on the part of Roman Catholics, especially American Roman Catholics.

Pope Paul VI formed the Pontifical Commission on the Study of Women in Society and in the Church, which operated between 1974 and 1976.[63] The year 1975, a Holy Year, was also declared as International Women's Year by the United Nations. In fact, during the mid-1970s there were multiple Curial efforts directed

---

[63]Marie-Thérèse van Lunen-Chenu, "La Commission Pontificale de la Femme: Une occasion manquée," *Études* 344 (1976): 879–91. She notes the failure of the Commission to achieve the goals set by the Third and Fourth Synods (1971 and 1974) in analyzing women's participation and responsibilities in the Catholic Church, and particularly the Commission's inadequacy for the task: "Pour constituer un essai de réelle collaboration et de participation des femmes à la vie communautaire de l'Église, la Commission de la femme a manqué de la liberté requise. Outre qu'elle disposa de moyens trop limités, il semble surtout que sa structure comme sa mission étaient fondamentalement inadéquates à la question posée."

at women. Among them, the Congregation for the Evangelization of Peoples conducted a study on "The Role of Women in
Evangelization," creating the postconciliar document published
as *Dans le cadre* ("In the context of the International Women's
Year...").[64] The study was a specifically pastoral commission, and
thereby restricted itself to what it saw as the apostolic work of
women rather than the ministerial work of women.[65] Meanwhile,
the International Theological Commission prepared a study on
"Women in the Diaconate," which was never released, the Biblical Commission presented a document entitled "Can Women Be
Priests?" which concluded that the New Testament could not provide a definitive answer to the question, and Father Louis Ligier of
the Congregation for the Doctrine of the Faith drafted a document
that came to be known as *Inter Insigniores*.[66] The Congregation
for the Doctrine of the Faith prepared *Inter Insigniores* without
consulting the International Theological Commission.[67]

Recent Church documents support the Church's understanding of a male-only priesthood.

Inter Insigniores, the Congregation for the Doctrine of the Faith's
1976 "Declaration on the Question of Admission of Women to
the Ministerial Priesthood" dated October 15 — the feast of
St. Teresa of Avila — of that year, presents the relative arguments accepted then by Paul VI, and since then by John Paul II
and, presumably although not definitively, by John Paul I, regard-

---

[64]In Austin Flannery, O.P., ed., *Vatican Council II: More Postconciliar Documents* (Leominster: Fowler, Wright, 1982), 2:318–30.

[65]In this construct, and for the most part, "apostolic" work seems to be traditionally diaconal work of service and "ministerial" work seems to be linked to sacramental and juridical structures of the Church.

[66]See Peter Hebblethwaite, *Paul VI: The First Modern Pope* (Mahwah, N.J.: Paulist Press, 1993), 640.

[67]Thomas P. Rausch, S.J., "Archbishop Quinn's Challenge: A Not Impossible Task" in *The Exercise of the Primacy: Continuing the Dialogue*, ed. Phyllis Zagano and Terrence W. Tilley (New York: Crossroad, 1998), 74–78, 79. Rausch notes that the Congregation for the Doctrine of the Faith failed to consult the International Theological Commission for at least three of its documents at this time: *Mysterium Ecclesiae* (1973), *Persona Humana* (1975), and *Inter Insigniores* (1977), and cites Francis A. Sullivan, "Authority in an Ecclesiology of Communion," *New Theology Review* 10, no. 3 (1997): 27–28.

ing the ordination of women to priesthood. *Inter Insigniores* came in the midst of ecumenical discussions between Rome and Canterbury, and the increasing acceptance of women priests by the Anglican communion may have caused what some commentators have seen as a "nonabsolutist tone" to *Inter Insigniores*. Significantly, *Inter Insigniores* does not reject the Anglican precedent of ordaining women, either to the diaconate or to the priesthood, nor does it state that the Catholic practice of not ordaining women is *de jure divino,* hence apparently allowing for continued discussion between and among communions that did and did not ordain women. Significantly, the official document emanating from the 1978 Anglican–Roman Catholic Versailles Conversation on the ordination of women confirmed that *Inter Insigniores* did not state that the prohibition against women priests was of divine law.[68]

The recognition of the dignity of women and of the possibility of their accession to office within and without the Church was widespread in the wake of International Woman's Year. The topic had been building within and without the Church for many years.[69] The role of women in Christian society had begun to be recognized with John XXIII's *Pacem in Terris,* in Vatican II's *Gaudium et Spes,* and in other statements and commentaries. The obviousness of the Church's need to declare the equality of men and women before God — in addition to the question of Anglican–Roman Catholic dialogue — lent a specific urgency to the "Declaration on the Question of the Admission of Women to the Ministerial Priesthood," and, coming as it did on the media heels of statements against the use of artificial means to limit births, it provided a second intellectual shoe to drop on the matter of women in the Church in a clearly unintended manner. Public comment and the way statements on these two matters were received via the media

---

[68]Christopher Hill, "The Ordination of Women and Anglican–Roman Catholic Dialogue," in *Women Priests?* ed. Alyson Peberdy (London: Marshall Pickering, 1988), 1–11.

[69]Most major writing began in the 1970s, although documents relating to widows, virgins, and deaconesses were collected in the mid-1930s. See Josephine Mayer, *Monumenta de viduis diaconissis virginibusque tractantia* (Bonn: P. Hanstein, 1938).

combined to inflict more damage to the magisterial teaching of the Church — or at least to the ability of the Church to teach magisterially — than any other event or events. The general (mediated) perception was of a split between women and those who appear to understand the needs and roles of women in modern society, and Church authority as an entity seeking to impose unnecessary limits on women's roles and overall freedoms.

The document itself garnered widespread media attention and significant scholarly responses, books, and essays.[70] The controversy raged, ebbed, and raged again, and the teaching Church adopted what some scholars regard as a highly defensive and rigid attitude on the matter..[71] The discussion led to the creation of another statement on the ordination of women to priesthood, this one by John Paul II. His Apostolic letter *Ordinatio Sacerdotalis* (1994) is supported by the earlier *Inter Insigniores* (1976). The titles of the documents indicate their increasing firmness: the first document, *Inter Insigniores*, is "On the Question of the Admission of Women to the Ministerial Priesthood"; the second document, *Ordinatio Sacerdotalis*, is "On Reserving Priestly Ordination to Men Alone."

The later *Ordinatio Sacerdotalis*, in turn, was the focus of such additional controversy that the Congregation for the Doctrine of the Faith declared it, although it did not call the prohibition

---

[70]Since the promulgation of *Inter Insigniores,* over 650 scholarly articles and 40 monographs have been catalogued on the subject "Ordination of Women–Catholic Church."

[71]The document *Inter Insigniores* was criticized by numerous scholars for its method and scholarship as well as its conclusions. For example, the New Testament references are considered anachronistic (John P. Meier, "On the Veiling of Hermeneutics [1 Cor. 11:2–16]," *Catholic Biblical Quarterly* 40:2 [1978]: 212–26); the patristic references in the document in their contexts apparently have nothing to do with ordaining women to priesthood (John K. Coyle, "Fathers on Women and Women's Ordination," *Église et Théologie* 9 [January 1978]: 51–101); the medieval references and their interpretations are questioned (Philip Lyndon Reynolds, "Scholastic Theology and the Case against Women's Ordination," *Heythrop Journal* 36, no. 3 [1995]: 249–85); and the iconic argument is challenged (Normand Provencher, "Église et sacerdoce ministériel," *Église et Théologie* 9, no. 1 [1978]: 209–21). "Women and Priestly Ministry: The New Testament Evidence," in *The Catholic Biblical Quarterly* 41 (1979): 608–13, prepared by seven members of the Catholic Biblical Association of America, roundly criticized the document. See also Wendell E. Langley and Rosemary Jermann, "Women and the Ministerial Priesthood: An Annotated Bibliography," *Theology Digest* 29 (Winter 1981): 329–42.

de jure divino, nevertheless to be part of the immutable deposit
of faith, and thereby an infallible teaching of the Holy See.
Then the apparent declaration of infallibility by the Congregation for the Doctrine of the Faith caused additional controversy
and debate.[72]

Independent of the issue of infallibility, the two documents,
Inter Insigniores (1976) and *Ordinatio Sacerdotalis* (1994), together
comprise the position presently held as regards the ordination of
women to priesthood. Each speaks only to the point of priestly
ordination. *Inter Insigniores,* as noted above, specifically excludes
discussion of ordination of women to the diaconate. *Ordinatio
Sacerdotalis,* the more recent of the two, seems to be directed
specifically at theological and popular discussion relative to the
possibility of admitting women to priesthood. In this latter letter, the Pope declares in the first person: "I declare that the
Church has no authority whatsoever to confer priestly ordination on women and this judgment is to be definitively held by all
the Church's faithful."[73]

As such, the latter letter can also be seen to be a supporting
document for the former. *Ordinatio Sacerdotalis* adds no new evidence or analysis of fact, and its brevity marks it as a declaration
of final support to the 1976 document, although it calls to the
prior letter for authority. The latter 1994 document was further
declared an infallible document by the Congregation for the Doctrine of the Faith, but, as noted above, most scholars dismiss this
declaration of infallibility as an interpretation of John Paul II's
intent rather than a clarification of it. No Pope has declared this
teaching infallible, and no teaching is held to be infallible unless
it is clearly stated as such. The two documents serve as overlays
of the arguments against the ordination of women to priesthood,
and the strength of each supports the notion of ordaining women
to the diaconate.

---

[72]Ladislas Orsy, "The Congregation's 'Response': Its Authority and Meaning," *America*
173, no. 19 (December 9, 1995): 4, typifies the debate.

[73]John Paul II, Apostolic letter *Ordinatio Sacerdotalis* (May 22, 1994), no. 4.

In 1976, Inter Insigniores *responded to calls for the ordination of women priests.*

Inter Insigniores has a brief introductory section on the role of women in society and in the Church, and argues in six parts against the ordination of women to priesthood: (1) the Church's Constant Tradition (ordaining only men to priesthood); (2) the Attitude of Christ (who chose only male apostles); (3) the Practice of the Apostles (who did not include women in their number); (4) the Permanent Value of the Attitude of Christ and the Apostles (establishing a permanent norm); (5) the Ministerial Priesthood in the Light of the Mystery of Christ (the priest must bear a "natural resemblance" to Christ); and, (6) the Ministerial Priesthood Illustrated by the Mystery of the Church (contemporary issues of gender equality are irrelevant).

Inter Insigniores presents the nonordination of women to priesthood as part of the Church's constant tradition, flowing from the attitude of Christ and the practice of the apostles, and then presents their acts as permanently binding. Two final sections expand sacramental theology to include the necessity of a physical resemblance to Christ, not so much in order to receive the sacrament of orders, but in order to act as a priest *in persona Christi* (the iconic argument). The document ends with the male priesthood as part and parcel of the mystery of the Church, despite any calls of contemporary society to the contrary.

The demonstration of the teaching against the ordination of women to priesthood flows from the concept of authority for acts as received from Christ. *Inter Insigniores* notes that changing roles of women mark a point that requires the Church to reevaluate the ways in which women are incorporated into it and the ways in which women serve. At the outset, however, the document presents the ordination of only men to priesthood as part of its constant tradition, stating, "The Catholic Church has never felt that priestly or episcopal ordination can be validly conferred on women" and it specifically states that those women who were ordained priests in the early Church belonged to heretical sects,

particularly Gnostic sects.[74] Although *Inter Insigniores* does not
deal specifically with the validity or invalidity of their ordination,
the document further states that the question of the ordination
of women to priesthood, while apparently disputed in the early
Church, was put to rest during medieval times and, "since that
period and up to our own time, it can be said that the question has
not been raised again, for the practice [of ordaining solely men to
priesthood] has enjoyed peaceful and universal acceptance."[75]

Inter Insigniores presents the argument (again, here only about
ordination to priesthood) that the Church has not sought to comment in succeeding centuries because the practice was universally
accepted. The role of women in society during these centuries
was in general not such that would support any notion of a female priesthood, so Church authority obviously did not comment
on the question again because it believed it did not have to.

The point of the commentary under discussion with *Inter
Insigniores* was to specifically argue against women priests, so apparently the need did arise, and strongly so. All its injunctions
and examples relate specifically to priesthood and revolve around
the testimony that Jesus did not entrust the apostolic charge
to women, and this attitude of Jesus and the apostles is to be
considered a permanent one for the Church.

The discussion in this document then turns to sacramental theology. The movement from sacrament as "sign" to the recipient
and effector of sacrament as "sign" is here complete. The document states that the person receiving the sacrament is part of the
matter of the sacrament,[76] and quotes Pius XII and the Council

---

[74]*Inter Insigniores*, no. 1.

[75]Ibid.

[76]Some argue that it is impossible for anyone to read this as anything other than
a statement that the female person is "defective matter," for this sacrament, as Thomas
Aquinas implied (*Summa Theologica* I, q. 92, arts. 1, 2; q. 93, art. 4), and therefore unable
to fully represent Christ. The document seems to present sex as substance, not accident,
in the matter of the person, that is, intrinsic to the makeup of the human who, when of
one sex or another, may be equal but not the same. This concept goes far deeper than the
iconic argument. It also incorrectly presents gender (as opposed to the imposition of hands
alone) as matter for the sacrament. Aquinas (or Rainaldo da Piperno, who constructed
the Supplement after Aquinas's death) considered the female sex to be an impediment to
the sacrament of orders (*Summa Theologica*, Supplement to III, q. 39, art. 1).

of Trent, thusly: "The Church has no power over the substance of
the sacraments, that is to say, over what Christ the Lord, as the
sources of revelation bear witness, determined should be maintained in the sacramental sign" (Pius XII, *Sacramentum Ordinis,*
1947),[77] and

> In the Church there has always existed this power, that in the
> administration of the sacraments, provided that their substance
> remains unaltered, she can lay down or modify what she con-
> siders more fitting either for the benefit of those who receive
> them or for respect towards those same sacraments, according
> to varying circumstances, times, or places.[78]

Therefore, the document affirms that the Church, while it is able
to accommodate particular circumstances, cannot change the nature and substance of any sacrament, and it explicitly considers the
male sex necessary to the substance of the sacrament of priestly
orders.

The document further states, "The Christian priesthood is
therefore of a sacramental nature: the priest is a sign, the super-
natural effectiveness of which comes from the ordination received,
but a sign that must be perceptible and which the faithful must
be able to recognize with ease."[79]

This statement includes an inherent notion that women do
not represent Christ, cannot represent Christ, that Christ cannot
be seen within women and therefore (obviously unintentionally)
that women do not represent, cannot represent, the promise or
the hope of the Incarnation or of the Resurrection. The implication that the faithful cannot recognize Christ "with ease" within

---

[77]*Inter Insigniores,* no. 4, fn. 13, citing Pope Pius XII, Apostolic Constitution
Sacramentum Ordinis, November 30, 1947; *Acta Apostolicae Sedis* 40 (1948): 5.

[78]*Inter Insigniores,* no. 4, citing the Council of Trent, session 21, chap. 2, Denzinger-
Schönmetzer, *Enchiridion Symbolorum,* 1728. This latter statement seems to indicate that
the Church does indeed have the authority to alter the "sign," perhaps even of maleness
and femaleness as they are presently considered.

[79]*Inter Insigniores,* no. 5, fn. 18, citing Thomas Aquinas: "For since a sacrament is a
sign, there is required in the things that are done in the sacraments not only the 'res' but
the signification of the 'res,' " recalls St. Thomas, precisely in order to reject the ordination
of women: *In IV Sent.,* dist. 25, q. 2, art. 1, quaestiuncula 1, corp. (p. 524).

a female, particularly a female celebrator of reconciliation or of Eucharist, led at least one American archbishop to suggest that the document calls the whole Church to "prayerful reflection on the meaning of such realities as priesthood, ministry, sacrament and the church itself."[80]

But the document is really arguing for the priest as "symbol," heavily supporting and being supported by the iconic argument relative to priesthood. *Inter Insigniores* further states that "the whole sacramental economy is in fact based upon natural signs, on *symbols* imprinted on the human psychology"[81] requiring "natural resemblance." And, again:

> The same natural resemblance is required for persons as for things: when Christ's role in the eucharist is to be expressed sacramentally, there would not be this "natural resemblance" which must exist between Christ and his minister if the role were not taken by a man: in such a case it would be difficult to see in the minister the image of Christ. For Christ himself was and remains a man.[82]

This sentence is immediately followed by:

> Christ is of course the firstborn of all humanity, of women as well as men: the unity which he re-established after sin is such that there are no more distinctions between Jew and Greek, slave and free, male and female, but all are one in Christ Jesus (cf. Gal. 3:28). Nevertheless, the incarnation of the word took place according to the male sex: this is indeed a question of fact, and this fact, while not implying an alleged natural superiority of man over woman, cannot be disassociated from the economy of salvation: it is, indeed, in harmony with the entirety of God's plan as God himself has revealed it, and of which the mystery of the covenant is the nucleus.[83]

---

[80]Cincinnati Archbishop Joseph Bernardin, then president of the National Conference of Catholic Bishops and later to become Cardinal Archbishop of Chicago. Margin Note, *Origins* 6, no. 33 (February 3, 1977): 520–21, 521.

[81]Emphasis added.

[82]*Inter Insigniores*, no. 5.

[83]Ibid.

In such the document seems to argue against itself, but not if we separate the dual uses of the term "sign" and replace the second use with the term "symbol." That is, again, the "sign" points to a fact and is a representation of it; the sacrament as sign signifies the fact of the reception of grace. The "symbol" encompasses the fact (including the "sign") and in actuality represents it. So the Church argues that women can neither be sign nor symbol of Christ in the sacramental economy of the celebration of the Eucharist, hence the ineligibility of women for priestly ordination.

Even so, the movement of *Inter Insigniores,* from quoting Thomas Aquinas ("Sacramental signs represent what they signify by natural resemblance") to immediately determining that "the same natural resemblance is required for persons as for things," does not extend to the fact of orders, but merely to a function of orders: specifically, "when Christ's role in the Eucharist is to be expressed sacramentally." It would follow, granting this, that only priesthood, which requires the function of celebrating Eucharist, requires the natural resemblance.

Another objection answered in *Inter Insigniores* is the understanding that the priest acts on behalf of the whole Church: "In this sense, the theologians of the Middle Ages said that the minister also acts *in persona Ecclesiae,* that is to say, in the name of the whole church and in order to represent her."[84] That the deacon more clearly acts *in persona Ecclesiae* (*in nomine Ecclesiae Christi*) argues to the diaconate being fully incorporated into the priesthood. The priest as well represents the whole Church as representative of Christ, the head and shepherd of the whole Church. Hence, the iconic argument here, too, presents the consistency of the Church's understandings.

A final section of *Inter Insigniores* discusses the question of human rights as regards priesthood, noting the distinction between the Church and other human societies. The Church's organization, it states, is specifically connected to orders:

---

[84] *Inter Insigniores,* no. 5.

The pastoral charge in the church is normally linked to the sacrament of order: it is not a simple government, comparable to the modes of authority found in states...it is the Holy Spirit, given by ordination, who grants participation in the ruling power of the supreme pastor, Christ (cf. Acts 20:28). It is a charge of service and love: "If you love me, feed my sheep" (cf. Jn. 21:15–17).[85]

Here the document appears to be more concerned with the office of bishop, as it relates to the sacrament of orders and the rank of priest, although "participation in the ruling power of the supreme pastor" would ordinarily flow to and through the bishop of a diocese to the pastors of the diocesan and territorial parishes. This is noted here because of the juridical distinctions between clerics and lay persons: some offices can only be held by those ordained to priesthood, many more only by those who are clerics, and some others require no ordination.

Scholarly and popular writing in response to *Inter Insigniores* continued. As noted above, many scholars and scholarly organizations found flaws in the theology of *Inter Insigniores,* and popular writers found even more flaws in its intent. What seems at the root of the discussion is whether the Church will entrust two sacraments, that of Eucharist and that of reconciliation, to women.

The report of the Pontifical Biblical Commission,[86] published prior to *Inter Insigniores,* presented the biblical discussion relative to women's ministry as it specifically related to priesthood. The seventeen members of the Pontifical Biblical Commission voted unanimously that the New Testament alone seemed unable to settle the question of the possibility of women priests, and the members voted 12–5 that scripture alone was not sufficient to rule out the admission of women to priesthood. The Pontifical Biblical

---

[85] *Inter Insigniores,* no. 6. At present the clerical state is tied to "order," whereas in the 1917 Code of Canon Law in force in 1977 all that was required for entry to the clerical state was tonsure, or the promise of the intent to be ordained. Juridical power is shared ordinarily and principally by those in the clerical state.

[86] "Can Women Be Priests?" Report of the Pontifical Biblical Commission, *Origins* 5 (July 1, 1976): 92–96.

Commission document, published as "Can Women Be Priests?" concludes:

> Is it possible that certain circumstances can come about which call on the church to entrust in the same way to certain women some sacramental ministries?
>
> This has been the case with baptism which, though entrusted to the apostles (Mt. 28:19 and Mk. 16:15f) can be administered by others as well. We know that at least later, it will be entrusted to women.
>
> Is it possible that we will come to this even with the ministry of eucharist and reconciliation which manifest eminently the service of the priesthood of Christ carried out by the leaders of the community?
>
> It does not seem that the New Testament by itself alone will permit us to settle in a clear way and once and for all the problem of the possible accession of women to the presbyterate.
>
> However, some think that in the scriptures there are sufficient indications to exclude this possibility, considering that the sacraments of eucharist and reconciliation have a special link with the person of Christ and therefore with the male hierarchy, as borne out by the New Testament. Others, on the contrary, wonder if the church hierarchy, entrusted with the sacramental economy, would be able to entrust the ministries of eucharist and reconciliation to women in light of circumstances, without going against Christ's original intentions.[87]

The questioning came to a halt, or perhaps was thought to have come to a halt, with the publication of *Inter Insigniores*. Like all Church documents, *Inter Insigniores* is designed to present the definitive argument of tradition illustrated by theology. But here the definitive argument apparently rested in the iconic argument: women could not represent Christ. Once granting this point, *Inter Insigniores* supports it by citing in a footnote other documents on priesthood:

Second Vatican Council, dogmatic constitution *Lumen Gentium*, 28: "Exercising within the limits of their authority the

---

[87]"Can Women Be Priests?" 96.

function of Christ as shepherd and head"; decree *Presbytero-rum Ordinis*, 2: "that they can act in the person of Christ the head"; 6: "the office of Christ the head and the shepherd." Cf. Pope Pius XII, encyclical letter *Mediator Dei*, "the minister of the altar represents the person of Christ as the head, offer-ing in the name of all his members": AAS 39 (1947), p. 556; 1971 Synod of Bishops, *De Sacerdotio Ministerali*, I, 4 "(The priestly ministry) . . . makes Christ, the head of the community, present."[88]

The argument in this respect appears to become circular, and some might say patronizing of women, because it again reduces to women not being able to represent Christ. As noted earlier, both scholarly and popular responses grew, and throughout the ensuing decades the question was more debated than before. Many of the proponents viewed the Pontifical Biblical Commission's "Can Women Be Priests?" as a hopeful sign that selective ordinations to priestly ministry might take place.

In 1994, Ordinatio Sacerdotalis *sought to end any discussion about women priests.*

The document *Inter Insigniores* did not stop continued theoretical and practical appeals for the ordination of women to priesthood. Because of the ensuing discussion, conjoined with the reports of secret priestly ordination of and ministry by five or six women in Czechoslovakia,[89] in 1994 Pope John Paul II issued the second document, "Apostolic Letter on Reserving Priestly Ordination to

---

[88]*Inter Insigniores*, no. 5, fn. 21. There is no thought here that a woman could be the head of a mixed community.

[89]Ludmila Javorova was reportedly ordained priest in 1970, and possibly bishop in the mid- to late 1980s, and ministered secretly under communist repression until 1989. "Miss Javorova told Vienna's Catholic magazine *Kirche Intern* she was one of several women priests working for Bishop Felix Davidek, the key leader of the underground movement established after the Red Army's tanks rolled into Czechoslovakia in 1968 to crush the Prague Spring. Bishop Davidek . . . organized the secret ordination and consecration of priests and bishops for fear that the clergy and the church would be eliminated by the communists. Of some three hundred secret clergy, about fifty were believed to be mar-ried male priests, two married male bishops, and several women priests." Women priests were apparently also ordained in Slovakia, by Bishop Nikolaus Krett. Ian Traynor, "Czech Woman Priest Emerges from Shadows," *Manchester Guardian*, November 11, 1995.

Men Alone," *Ordinatio Sacerdotalis.* This brief letter refers to the discussion that existed prior to *Inter Insigniores,* and then reviews its basic arguments. The reasons noted in the first section of *Ordinatio Sacerdotalis* are taken from a 1975 letter of Pope Paul VI to the Archbishop of Canterbury:

> ...the example recorded in Sacred Scriptures of Christ choosing his Apostles only from among men; the constant practice of the Church, which has imitated Christ in choosing only men; and her living teaching authority which has constantly held that the exclusion of women from the priesthood is in accordance with God's plan for his Church.[90]

The discussion that ensues is not a complete one, but a reaffirmation of teachings and statements promulgated in and after 1975. Scripture is used to document the notion that Christ chose only male apostles, and the apostles chose only men, but passages noted by the Pontifical Biblical Commission to suggest that, if not Christ, at least possibly the apostles chose women to share in their apostolic ministry are not mentioned. The document "Can Women Be Priests?" of the Pontifical Biblical Commission is neither referred to nor explicitly refuted by *Ordinatio Sacerdotalis,* which, citing 1 Timothy 3:1–13, 2 Timothy 1:6, and Titus 1:5–9 states that Christ chose only men and "the Apostles did the same when they chose fellow workers who would succeed them in their ministry."[91] (The Pontifical Biblical Commission had cited 1 Timothy 3:1–13 in support of women as "fellow workers," in this case as deacons.) The Pontifical Biblical Commission's comments on women having possibly attained an equivalent priesthood as it is projected to the time of the apostles is not referred to by *Ordinatio Sacerdotalis.* Yet the Pontifical Biblical Commission's exegesis is explicit:

---

[90]*Ordinatio Sacerdotalis,* no. 1, citing Paul VI, Response to the Letter of His Grace the Most Reverend Dr. F. D. Coggan, Archbishop of Canterbury, concerning the Ordination of Women to Priesthood (November 30, 1975), *Acta Apostolicae Sedis* 68 (1976): 599. The prefatory language to this sentence indicates that the Catholic Church would consider Anglican ordination of women priests a barrier to Christian unity.

[91]*Ordinatio Sacerdotalis,* no. 2.

Some women collaborated in the properly apostolic work. This is shown at numerous points in the Acts and the epistles. We shall limit ourselves to a few of them.

In the establishment of local communities, they are not content with offering their houses for meetings, as Lydia (Acts 16, 14–15), the mother of Mark (Acts 12,12), Prisca (Rom. 16,5), but, according to Phil. 4,2, for example, Evodia and Syntyche are explicitly associated with "Clement and the other collaborators of Paul" in the community. Of the 27 persons thanked or greeted by Paul in the last chapter of the Epistle to the Romans, nine or perhaps 10 are women. In the case of several of them, Paul insists on specifying that they have tired themselves for the community, using a Greek verb (*kopian*) most often used for the work of evangelization properly so called.

.... Also notable is the case of Junias or Junio, placed in the rank of the apostles (Rom. 16,7), with regard to whom one or another raises the question of whether it is a man.[92]

The Responsum ad Dubium *states that* Ordinatio Sacerdotalis *is part of the deposit of faith.*

That theologians did not stop discussing the ordination of women to priesthood at the publication of *Ordinatio Sacerdotalis* in mid-1994 generated an unusually swift reaction from Joseph Cardinal Ratzinger, prefect of the Congregation for the Doctrine of the Faith. In the fall of 1995, he published two documents, a brief one entitled "Sacred Congregation for the Doctrine of the Faith on *Ordinatio Sacerdotalis, Responsum ad Dubium,*" which states that the reply was approved by John Paul II, and a longer explanation of the *Responsum ad Dubium,* which was not. The brief papal-approved *Responsum ad Dubium* is as follows:

> *Dubium:* Whether the teaching that the Church has no authority whatsoever to confer priestly ordination on women, which is presented in the Apostolic letter *Ordinatio Sacerdotalis* to be held definitively, is to be understood as belonging to the deposit of faith.

---

[92]"Can Women Be Priests?" 95.

Responsum: In the affirmative.

This teaching requires definitive assent, since, founded on the written Word of God, and from the beginning constantly preserved and applied in the Tradition of the Church, it has been set forth infallibly by the ordinary and universal Magisterium (cf. Second Vatican Council, Dogmatic Constitution on the Church *Lumen Gentium* 25, 2). Thus, in the present circumstances, the Roman Pontiff, exercising his proper office of confirming the brethren (cf. Lk. 22:32), has handed on this same teaching by a formal declaration, explicitly stating what is to be held always, everywhere, and by all, as belonging to the deposit of the faith.

The Sovereign Pontiff John Paul II, at the Audience granted to the undersigned Cardinal Prefect, approved this Reply, adopted in the ordinary session of the Congregation, and ordered it to be published.[93]

The statement above was joined and supported by a fifteen-hundred-word statement by Joseph Cardinal Ratzinger alone (i.e., not approved by the Pope), which states that the teaching that the Church does not have the authority to ordain women to priesthood is "a doctrine taught infallibly by the Church." The operative paragraph reads as follows:

In response to this precise act of the Magisterium of the Roman Pontiff, explicitly addressed to the entire Catholic Church, all members of the faithful are required to give their assent to the teaching stated therein. To this end, the Congregation for the Doctrine of the Faith, with the approval of the Holy Father, has given an official Reply on the nature of this assent; it is a matter of full definitive assent, that is to say, irrevocable, to a doctrine taught infallibly by the Church. In fact, as the Reply explains, the definitive nature of this assent derives from the truth of the doctrine itself, since, founded on the written Word of God, and constantly held and applied in the Tradition of

---

[93] Joseph Cardinal Ratzinger, "Sacred Congregation for the Doctrine of the Faith, On *Ordinatio Sacerdotalis*, Responsum ad Dubium," October 28, 1995.

the Church, it has been set forth infallibly by the ordinary universal Magisterium (cf. *Lumen Gentium, 25*). Thus, the Reply
specifies that this doctrine belongs to the deposit of the faith
of the Church. It should be emphasized that the definitive and
infallible nature of this teaching of the Church did not arise
with the publication of the Letter *Ordinatio Sacerdotalis*. In the
Letter, as the Reply of the Congregation of the Doctrine of the
Faith also explains, the Roman Pontiff, having taken account
of present circumstances, has confirmed the same teaching by
a formal declaration, giving expression once again to *quod sem-
per, quod ubique et quod ab omnibus tenendum est, utpote ad fidei
depositum pertinens*. In this case, an act of the ordinary papal
Magisterium, in itself not infallible, witnesses to the infallibility
of the teaching of a doctrine already possessed by the Church.[94]

The locutions of this document really only served to make it even
more dubious to its critics.[95] Were the Pope to state, simply so that
all might understand, that the current teaching that women may
not be ordained priests is infallibly true, the Church might not be
engaged even now in continued theological discussion exemplified
above and continued on both sides. Each of these two statements
by Cardinal Ratzinger fanned the argumentative fires even more,
with numerous individual theologians and theological assemblies
disagreeing, now not only with the teaching on the ordination of
women to priesthood but also with the statement by the prefect of
the Congregation for the Doctrine of the Faith that this teaching
is infallible.

---

[94]Joseph Cardinal Ratzinger, "Concerning the CDF Reply Regarding *Ordinatio Sacerdotalis*," October 28, 1997. "...what always, everywhere, and by everyone ought to be
held as pertaining to the deposit of faith").

[95]There was major public discussion of the document and the statement by the
Congregation for the Doctrine of the Faith in the media: see "Rules Stay the Same:
Men Only, Vatican Says Cardinal Reaffirms Church's Position," *St. Louis Post-Dispatch*,
November 19, 1995; "Vatican Panel Hardens Ban on Women Priests," *Washington Post*,
November 19, 1995; Philip Pullella, "Vatican Emphatic against Women Priests," *Detroit
News*, November 19, 1995; "World-wide: The Vatican Tried to Halt Debate," *Wall Street
Journal*, November 20, 1995; John Hooper, "Vatican Move on 'Men-Only' Rule Hinders
Hopes of Christian Unity," *Manchester Guardian*, November 20, 1995; Virginia Culver,
"Vatican Ban on Female Priests Sparks Angry Reaction," *Denver Post*, November 18, 1995;
Jerry Filteau, "Papal No to Women Priests Is Infallible, Document Says" *National Catholic
Reporter*, December 1, 1995.

The newly-raised claim that the teaching regarding women priests is an infallible teaching caused specific discussion about the nature of infallibility. Canonist Ladislas Orsy denied any interpretation of the combined effects of the papal or Congregation for the Doctrine of the Faith's statements that would lead to a determination of infallibility, noting that a "special approval" to the Congregation's *Responsum* would be required:

> The present document does not speak of "special approval," nor does it carry any expression equivalent to "special"; hence, by the rule of law, the conclusion must be that it has the authority of the congregation, no less and no more.
>
> Such an authority does not include infallibility. The reason for this is theological. Infallibility cannot be delegated. It is a charism granted to the pope (as well as to the episcopal college and to the universal body of the faithful); no other office or body in the church can possess it. The assistance of the Holy Spirit cannot be transferred....
>
> A nonfallible organ of the Holy See, on its own authority, does not have the power to modify in any way the doctrinal weight of a papal pronouncement. It has, however, the right to publish its own view, which must be received with the respect due to that office.[96]

Other scholars broadly discounted any claim to infallibility, especially in light of the fact that the claim was not being made by the Pope. The response of the Catholic Theological Society of America (CTSA) is similar to those by other major scholars and scholarly organizations. The CTSA appointed a Task Force chaired by Jon Nilson, Associate Professor of Theology at Loyola University of Chicago, to prepare a document on the ordination of women as priests, "Tradition and the Ordination of Women." The CTSA Board, on June 5, 1997, unanimously endorsed the conclusions of the paper, namely:

---

[96]Ladislas Orsy, "The Congregation's 'Response': Its Authority and Meaning," *America* 173, no. 19 (December 9, 1995): 4.

There are serious doubts regarding the nature of the authority of this teaching and its grounds in Tradition. There is serious, widespread disagreement on this question not only among theologians, but also within the larger community of the Church. Once again, its seems clear, therefore, that further study, discussion and prayer regarding this question by all members of the Church in accord with their particular gifts and vocations are necessary if the Church is to be guided by the Spirit in remaining faithful to the authentic Tradition of the Gospel in our day.[97]

The CTSA document, which was approved by a vote of 216 for, 22 against, 10 abstentions, created a further furor in Catholic circles, a furor marked by deep anger.[98]

It is a point of Canon Law that if something is not clearly infallible then it is not in fact infallible.[99] However, infallibly or not, the Church through papal documents has called the question of ordaining women to priesthood closed. If the Church believes the matter is closed, then there is no danger that women ordained deacons can be ordained priests. If this is to be definitively held,

---

[97] "Tradition and the Ordination of Women: CTSA Resolution," Catholic Theological Society of America, June 5, 1997.

[98] For example, Bernard Cardinal Law of Boston wrote: "The academic theological community has become victim to the various politically correct currents of academe.... The most recent expression of dereliction of responsibility on the part of the CTSA is not surprising. It was predictable. How would a group of authentic Catholic theologians address the Church's teaching on the ordination of women? For starters, the teaching itself would be a given. The difficulties it poses would be acknowledged. An effort would be made to elucidate the teaching.... What a wasteland is the professional Catholic theological community as represented by the CTSA." Bernard Cardinal Law, "The CTSA: A Theological Wasteland," *The Pilot,* June 18, 1997, http://www.rcab.org/pilotlaw/Column061897.html. In this column, Cardinal Law names those he would have preferred to have heard from on the matter of the ordination of women to priesthood within the Catholic Church, including a number of persons not known as Catholics: Father Avery Dulles, S.J. (Professor Emeritus of Theology, Catholic University and currently holding the Laurence J. McGinley Chair of Religion and Society at Fordham University), Sister Sara Butler, M.S.B.T., Mary Ann Glendon (Professor, Harvard Law School), Elizabeth Fox-Genovese (Professor of History, Emory University), Jean Bethke Elshtain (Laura Spelman Rockefeller Professor of Social and Political Ethics, University of Chicago Divinity School), Gertrude Himmelfarb (Professor Emeritus of History, City University of New York), and Barbara Dafoe Whitehead.

[99] Canon 747.3: "No doctrine is understood to be infallibly defined unless it is clearly established as such."

then, even if there is historical or theological doubt in the matter, no one should raise the possibility of women priests as an objection to ordaining women deacons.

Summary

The Church has given reasons why women, although ontologically equal to men, may not be ordained to priesthood. Closing priesthood to women does not preclude the diaconate for women, because diaconal orders do not imply priestly orders. Despite the fact that sacraments are essentially open to all human persons, Church teaching restricts priestly orders because of its understandings of sign and symbol. It is the Church that restricts priesthood to men, and Church authority's response to contemporary culture's arguments is still "no." Recent Church documents support the Church's understanding of a male-only priesthood: in 1976, *Inter Insigniores* responded to the calls for the ordination of women priests, and in 1994 *Ordinatio Sacerdotalis* sought to end any discussion about women priests. The *Responsum ad Dubium* states that *Ordinatio Sacerdotalis* is part of the deposit of faith.

III. The judgment that women cannot be ordained priests does not apply to the question of whether women can be ordained deacons.

Closing discussion relative to women priests opens the discussion relative to women deacons.

For Church authority to restrict the ability to celebrate Eucharist and to grant reconciliation to those whom it considers to be iconically acting *in persona Christi,* that is, validly ordained male priests, is to eliminate women from the possibility of celebrating these sacraments. The Church has stated that the matter is closed, insofar as ordaining women to priesthood is concerned. If the matter of the ordination of women to priesthood is definitively closed, even if the Church revisits its earlier understanding of its ability to ordain women to the diaconate, there would still remain these barriers to women celebrating these two sacraments. That is, *Inter Insigniores* and *Ordinatio Sacerdotalis* would remain in force.

If the teaching is to be definitively held, then all members of the Church must separate the possibility of ordaining women to priesthood from the possibility of ordaining women to the diaconate. Equally, all members of the Church must refuse the argument against ordaining women deacons that states if women can be ordained deacons then women can be ordained priests, because while women are ontologically equal to men, and can be ordained, the Church does not find it has the authority to ordain women to priesthood, nor does it believe that women can function iconically as priests, given the Church's understanding of the priest acting *in persona Christi.* To ordain women to the diaconate does not imply that the Church considers itself authorized to ordain women to priesthood.

Therefore, the question of whether women may be ordained to priesthood is irrelevant to the question of whether women may be ordained to the diaconate.

64

Diaconal orders are distinct from priestly orders.

Sacramental theology can argue that there is no separation of orders, that once ordained the ordinand is able to be advanced in rank, but the Church has always juridically restricted such advancement, and in fact has reinstated the diaconate and called it "permanent." There are other juridical restrictions to advancement within orders. For example, in the East, married men may not become bishops. In the West, married men may become priests only if they were previously ordained to ministry in another Christian denomination, but they may not become bishops so long as they are married. Also in the West, married men are ordained deacons without impediment ("permanent" deacons), but it is understood that they may not be ordained priests so long as they are married.

So the argument that once ordained deacons women would automatically be eligible for ordination to priesthood is specious, and, as regards women, directly insubordinate to the documents *Inter Insigniores* and *Ordinatio Sacerdotalis*.

Independent of arguments about the possibility of women being ordained to priesthood, there are obviously several other questions relative to orders that can be addressed specifically to the diaconate, particularly in the case of the possibility of the admission of women to the diaconate: Is the conferral of orders, specifically ordination to the diaconate, an occasion of communal acceptance of the ministry of the ordinand? Does the ordinand have the right to request orders, or must the community call the deacon forth? Does the work of the diaconate and the fact of ordination to it specifically exclude or specifically include the service of women?

The diaconate, which by the Middle Ages had been reduced to a step along the way toward ordination to the priesthood, and which fell into oblivion as a separate permanent order (Francis of Assisi and Alcuin are two notable exceptions), has been revived in the Church in modern times as a means of meeting the need for the ministry of the Church, that is, as a means of revitalizing the important ministerial duties given to deacons of the early Church.[100]

Given theological developments relative to the Church's understanding of priesthood specifically as a ministerial (as well as cultic) need and function of the Church, the arguments for an expanded diaconate — to provide for the ministry of the Church — begin to sound very close to the present understanding of priesthood. Therefore, if the work of the deacon is the same as the work of the priest, why not ordain women as deacons *and* as priests?

After all, it can be argued, priesthood cannot be restricted to its cultic Old Testament role and is therefore no longer dependent on or restricted by the iconic argument. The shift in the classical understanding of priest within the Church was noted by the International Theological Commission in 1970, not as a change in the way priesthood has been handed down over the centuries, but rather in the way it is presented in theology textbooks. That is, the theology of priesthood has not changed; the emphasis in its understanding has. From Trent to Vatican II, the Commission wrote, the status of the priest within the Church remained. He was administrator of sacraments and lived "sacerdotally," responsible for the unchanging doctrine of the Church and belonging to a special class. The Commission wrote:

> Vatican II has modified this priestly image in two respects. The Council has dealt with the common priesthood of all the faithful before treating of the ministerial priesthood, and the term "ministerial" has been added deliberately. It has, moreover, put in relief the place of the bishop, the center of the particular Church and member of the universal college of bishops. The place of the priest in the Church has thus become less clear.[101]

---

[100]The diaconate as a distinct vocation, not necessarily a step toward priesthood, flourished up to the fifth century. The Council of Trent proposed it be reestablished. It was finally restored in 1972. See Paul VI, Apostolic letter *Ad Pascendum* (August 15, 1972), and Congregation for Catholic Education and Congregation for the Clergy, *Basic Norms for the Formation of Permanent Deacons and Directory for the Ministry and Life of Permanent Deacons* (Washington, D.C.: United States Catholic Conference, 1998), 14–15.

[101]"The Priestly Ministry," approved as a working document by the International Theological Commission and prepared by a subcommittee headed by M.-J. Le Guillou with Hans Urs von Balthasar, Carlo Colombo, Gonzalez de Gardebal, Joseph Lescrauwaet, and

The lack of clarity the Commission saw retains its upsetting character today. What, exactly, is the distinction between priest and deacon? Obviously, the legalities and capacities regarding celebration of Eucharist, reconciliation, and anointing distinguish the sacramental faculties and function of the priest and deacon. But given, as the Commission wrote, "the ministry of the priest has become more diversified," the function of priest has broadened and it no longer suffices "for him to just perform sacramental functions and all that goes directly with them." This new understanding of priesthood is less from Old Testament cultic concepts and more from New Testament "presbyterial" concepts, replacing "power" with "charge" always in terms of a ministry of service.[102] That the priest responds to the sacramental needs of the community *in persona Christi* does not overcome the fact that he also responds *in nomine Christi* as well as *in nomine ecclesiae*. The service in the name of Christ and in the name of Christ by the Church, that is, all ministry, is done by those ordained and not ordained, male and female. Specific ministries, specific tasks of the Church, require orders. There is nothing about them that restricts the other work of the Church, ministry, which is *in nomine Christi* as well as *in nomine ecclesiae,* to men, be they priests or deacons. Hence there is nothing that would restrict the work of a restored female diaconate to complement priestly orders and ministries.

They who served as women deacons were indeed recognized as members of the roster of clergy, even though their descendants in the Roman Catholic Church today are not ordained. We know that women deacons were included in the roster of clergy because the Council of Nicea and succeeding councils ruled they could no longer be so included.[103] The diaconal ordination ceremony of the Apostolic Constitutions, codified by at least two councils (Nicea, 325, and Chalcedon, 451), signified the acceptance of the service of the ordinand (male or female) by the community, and there

---

J. Medina-Estevez in Michael Sharkey, ed., *International Theological Commission: Texts and Documents 1969–1985* (San Francisco: Ignatius Press, 1989), 9.

[102] Sharkey, *International Theological Commission,* 9.

[103] Joseph Martos, *Doors to the Sacred* (Garden City, N.Y.: Doubleday, 1981), 473.

were ceremonies extant and still found in the conciliar documents that present the ritual for the ordination of a deaconess.[104]

It is entirely possible that the reverse is true today. That is, the community accepts the service of the deacon that begins after ordination. Of course, diaconal training programs present the deacon-candidate as a minister, and deacon-candidates are often drawn from other ministries in the Church. Even so, rather than recognize what is already the fact, diaconal ordination creates a new one. But the new fact is not a fact of priesthood.

Women's ministry can be recognized as diaconal.

The contemporary restoration of the permanent diaconate raises a particular problem with the fact of women presently ministering in diaconal roles without ordination. The conferral of the diaconate (and subsequent granting of faculties) is restricted to the bishop of the diocese in which the ordinand serves.[105] Implicit is the fact that it is the bishop on behalf of the local Church (or major superior of a clerical religious institute or personal prelature) who calls the individual to ordained service.

Independent of this fact, the contemporary Church experiences and recognizes women's ministry, specifically including that which is otherwise named as diaconal service. Church authority has recognized needs that exceed those allowed for in current categories (lay ministers, catechists) or installed offices (lector, acolyte), and it in fact "calls forth" the service of women in many ways and through many specific ministries (chaplains to institutions, spiritual directors, pastoral associates, specific offices).[106] Yet there is

---

[104]Historical records are more fully discussed in a subsequent chapter. To be sure, there are other documents that argue against what seems to be the contemporary practice of ordaining women deacons. Several councils in the West argue against what seems to be the practice: Nîmes (396), Orange (441), Epaon (517), and Orléans (533). See Bradshaw, *Ordination Rites,* 83–92.

[105]A dimissorial letter from the diocesan bishop or major superior would allow for another bishop to perform the ceremony. See Canons 1018, 1019.

[106]Nonordained persons may not receive leadership titles, such as "pastor" or "chaplain." See art 1. of the Instruction "Some Questions Regarding Collaboration of Non-Ordained Faithful in Priests' Sacred Ministry," co-signed by the prefects of the Congregations for Clergy, Doctrine of the Faith, Divine Worship and Discipline of the Sacraments, Bishops, Evangelization of Peoples, Institutes of Consecrated Life and Soci-

still no way for the bishop of a diocese, on behalf of the local Church, to formally call forth women servants of the Church, to recognize and to ratify their service through orders. Hence the ministry of women can be argued to be extraneous, insofar as it is not recognized as intrinsic through orders. If ordination signifies both the calling forth and the sending forth of an individual in service to the Church, there will of needs be established a ritual by which an individual woman is bound to the Church that does not imply priesthood.[107] That ritual already exists: ordination to the diaconate.

If the candidate for ordination has the right to request orders, in accord with the call of the community, then it becomes incumbent upon those who have the authority to confer orders (an authority from Christ ratified by the Church as a whole) to seek to call all who have requested orders, if the act of ordination is to both signify and initiate diaconal service to the Church on the part of the individual. If the candidate does not have the right to request orders, it would appear even more pressing that the diocesan bishop find an ordinary means to provide for the needs of the local Church by calling forth those who appear to serve in the capacity of deacon to maintain the sacramental ministry (here specifically baptism and marriage) with which he as bishop is entrusted.[108]

---

eties of Apostolic Life, and the presidents of the Councils for the Laity and Interpretation of Legislative Texts. *Origins* 27, no. 24 (November 27, 1997): 403. In practice, however, many women in the employ of schools, prisons, and hospitals are called "chaplains" by their employers.

[107] In certain instances, the public vows of women religious were once considered public only where they were made in the presence of the diocesan bishop or his delegate and recorded in the proper location. "In some congregations, however, the constitutions prescribe that the profession be received, not by the superior, but by the Bishop or his delegate." Commentary on Canon 1308.1 (1917 Code) in T. Lincoln Bouscaren, A. C. Ellis, F. N. Korth, *Canon Law: A Text and Commentary*, 4th ed., rev. (Milwaukee: Bruce, 1966), 279. It would seem that this fact — recalling the Constitution *Conditae* of Leo XIII — is an additional vestige of the historical fact of women deacons and their ordination, that is, of their connection to the diocesan bishop. Additionally, profession of vows is noted on the back of baptismal certificates, just as are marriage and the reception of holy orders.

[108] That is, without needing to request rescripts for lay persons to solemnly baptize and witness marriages. "The ordinary minister of baptism is a bishop, presbyter or deacon..." (Canon 861); "Only those marriages are valid which are contracted in the presence of the

Orders are the only permanent means by which a diocesan bishop can call forth women in service.

One way of incorporating individuals into the public service of the Church is by religious profession of vows, and the major superior of a religious order or institute is the only person who can call forth individuals to this service and incorporation.[109] What means does the bishop of the diocese have to call forth women other than starting his own religious order, which in time will no longer be bound to the diocesan bishop?[110] Further, as priesthood is distinct from the diaconate, how does the bishop of the diocese provide for the needs of the people for diaconal service?

The bishops of the United States, in requesting permission to initiate the permanent diaconate in the United States, gave five specific reasons for the diaconate in this country:

- to enrich and strengthen the many and various diaconal ministries at work in this country with the sacramental grace of the diaconate;

- to enlist a new group of devout and competent men in the active ministry of the Church;

- to aid in extending needed liturgical and charitable services to the faithful in both large urban and small rural communities;

- to provide an official and sacramental presence of the Church in many areas of secular life, as well as in communities within large cities and sparsely settled regions where few or no priests are available;

---

local ordinary or the pastor or a priest or deacon delegated by either of them..." (Canon 1108.1). Lay persons can be delegated extraordinarily.

[109]Persons are admitted by the major superior (Canon 641) and incorporated by religious profession (Canon 654). As noted earlier, the 1917 Code effectively withdrew the right of the diocesan bishop to admit to a diocesan institute.

[110]Some diocesan bishops continue to found diocesan congregations of women. The Sisters of Life, founded by John Cardinal O'Connor of New York in 1992, is presently an association of the faithful (what was once known as a pious union). Interestingly, the Sisters of Life sit in the choir stalls of the main altar during the Cardinal's Sunday liturgy, a practice similar to that of ancient deaconesses.

- to provide an impetus and source for creative adaptations of diaconal ministries to the rapidly changing needs of our society.[111]

Obviously, these reasons can be equally applied to women. Since the Church chooses to retain the discipline of celibate male priesthood, which restricts priesthood by number and, ultimately, to its right and proper functions, the Church will of needs call forth others to serve in the diaconate, just as it presently calls forth men from the married state to be deacons (and, in some cases, priests). A woman cleric bound to the diocesan bishop might better safeguard the universality of his episcopacy, and better safeguard the Church's jurisdiction and sacraments, than a lay minister who has no specific two-way relationship with or commitment to the diocesan bishop.[112] Again, eliminating the possibility of priestly orders for women does not eliminate the possibility or need for the accession of women to the clerical state.

Ordained diaconal ministry is ministry of service.

A broader understanding of the implications and the possibilities of ordination of women to the diaconate might well enlighten the Church, whose ordained ministers are fewer and whose un-ordained servants are more numerous, and would underscore the fact that the objections to the ordination of women as priests are irrelevant to the question of women deacons. Nothing in the ministry of the deacon presupposes a sacrificial priesthood or the eligibility for it. Nothing in the ritual of ordination to the diaconate implies ordination to the sacrificial priesthood.[113]

As posited earlier, it is readily apparent that the work of the

---

[111]National Conference of Catholic Bishops, Committee on the Permanent Diaconate, *Permanent Deacons in the United States: Guidelines on Their Formation and Ministry*, rev. ed. (Washington, D.C.: National Conference of Catholic Bishops, 1984), 1–2. If "men" indeed means "all people," then women are already included in this English-language request.

[112]That is, who is by definition always merely a contractual employee of a diocese.

[113]*Lumen Gentium*, no. 29, cites *Constitutiones Ecclesiae aegyptiacae*, III, 2: ed. Funk, *Didascalia*, II, p. 103, and *Statuta Eccl. Ant.* 371: Mansi 3, 954: "At a lower level of the hierarchy are deacons, upon whom hands are imposed 'not unto the priesthood, but to ministry.'"

diaconate is specifically this: ministry to the Church. Beyond, that ministry to the Church does not exclude the service of women, but in fact includes such service. The increasing service of women in diaconal roles without their personal binding to the diocesan bishop creates a more scattered approach to the ministry of the local Church than is actually necessary. Lay ministers serving as "lay deacons" invite individual juridical and sacramental problems, which might be obviated by a return to the tradition of an ordained female diaconate. One would hope that a clearer understanding of the sacrament of orders, particularly diaconal orders, would encourage a revitalization of the diaconate's historic possibilities and future potential as a means of expanding the ministry of the women of the Church. As argued earlier, feminist theology that becomes a counter-ecclesiology creates arguments against itself, but feminist understandings of the ontological reality of the human person are powerful reminders of the pressing need the whole Church has for a restored female diaconate.

Thousands of women, religious and secular, have chosen to remain Catholic and serve the Church as lay ministers, and their service is applauded. It would seem that if women might experience a genuine vocation to lay ministry, women would equally be able to experience a genuine vocation to the diaconate.

Summary

Closing discussion relative to women priests opens the discussion relative to women deacons. Diaconal orders are distinct from priestly orders, and women's ministry can be recognized as diaconal. Orders are the only means by which a diocesan bishop can call forth a woman in service, and ordained diaconal ministry is a ministry of service. Hence, the judgment that women cannot be ordained priests does not apply to the question of whether women can be ordained deacons.

IV. Women are and have been called to the diaconate.

Liturgical restrictions may have clouded the role of women deacons.

Women have often been restricted from the liturgical ministries, but these restrictions are gradually eroding. The 1983 Code of Canon Law made an attempt to remove the divisions between lay men and lay women in service to the Church. The restriction against the installation of women as lectors or acolytes remains, but no such restriction legally exists against women performing the functions of lector or acolyte.[114] Those arguing (in English-speaking countries) that Canon 230.3 ("...lay persons, even if they are not lectors or acolytes, can also supply for certain of their offices") did not admit to altar service by women were simply translating *videlicet* restrictively, as "namely" instead of as "for example."[115] The final resolution in favor of women serving as acolytes by the Pontifical Council for the Interpretation of Legislative Texts was published by the Congregation for Divine Worship and Discipline of the Sacraments on March 15, 1994, although

---

[114]"Lay men...can be installed on a stable basis in the ministries of lector and acolyte..." (Canon 230.1). Note: this paragraph of the Canon calls for *Viri laici* — male lay persons. However, "Lay persons can fulfill the function of lector" (Canon 230.2) and "...lay persons, even if they are not lectors or acolytes, can also supply for certain of their offices" (Canon 230.3). The latter two paragraphs refer only to *laici*.

[115]The translation of *videlicet* as "namely" rather than as "for example" is in the 1983 Canon Law Society of America *Code of Canon Law, Latin-English Edition*, which received the Nihil Obstat from Bishop Anthony J. Bevilacqua, then chairman of the National Conference of Catholic Bishops' Canonical Affairs Committee.

Canon 230.1: "Viri laici, qui aetate dotibusque pollent Episcoporum conferentiae decreto statutis, per ritum liturgicum praescriptum ad ministeria lectoris et acolythi stabiliter assumi possunt; quae tamen ministeriorum collatio eisdem ius non confert ad sustentationem remunerationemve ab Ecclesia praestandam.

2. Laici ex temporanea deputatione in actionibus liturgicis munus lectoris implere possunt; item omnes laici muneribus commentatoris, cantoris aliisve ad normam iuris fungi possunt.

3. Ubi Ecclesiae necessitas id suadeat, deficientibus ministris, possunt etiam laici, etsi non sint lectores vel acolythi, quaedam eorundem officia supplere, videlicet ministerium verbi exercere, precibus liturgicis praeesse, baptismum conferre atque sacram Communionem distribuere, iuxta iuris praescripta."

no *right* to altar service can be imputed to women or to any other noncleric.[116]

Among the most obvious reasons to deny such altar service to women, even where expressly permitted by law, was the custom (or perhaps superstition) best explained by the prophet Ezekiel. "Thus the word of the Lord came to me: Son of man, when the house of Israel lived in their land, they defiled it by conduct and deeds. In my sight their conduct was like the defilement of a menstruating woman" (Ezek. 36:16–19). In the early Church, when women clearly served as deacons, there were implicit restrictions against those menstruating. The ordination of a woman to the diaconate was often withheld until she was at least forty, presumably enough time for her to have completed menstruation and therefore no longer to present the risk of defiling the sanctuary,[117] where she was allowed to enter it at all even if she was a deaconess.[118]

Such ancient superstition is echoed today by those who declare the unfitness of women for service. It stands as root to the argument that Phoebe of Romans 16, whom Paul called a deaconess, did not serve the Church as deacon.[119] Despite the distinct possi-

---

[116]Despite Canon 230's location within the section of Canon Law entitled "The Obligations and Rights of the Lay Christian Faithful," the letter of Antonio M. Cardinal Javierre Ortas, president of the Pontifical Council for the Interpretation of Texts, writes: "It must also be clearly understood that the liturgical services mentioned above are carried out by lay people *ex temporanea deputatione*, according to the judgement of the bishop, without lay people, be they men or women, having any right to exercise them." See "Use of Female Altar Servers Allowed," *Origins* 23, no. 45 (April 28, 1994): 777, 779. See also Pontifical Council for the Interpretation of Legislative Texts, "Responsio ad propositum dubium," June 30, 1992, *Acta Apostolicae Sedis* 86 (1994): 541–42.

[117]See especially the Canons regarding ordination of women to the diaconate from the Councils of Nicea and Chalcedon. The age restrictions for women deacons gradually dropped, from age sixty, to fifty, and, finally, to forty.

[118]Some ordination ceremonies distinguish the deacon and deaconess as regards liturgical ministry. For example, the Nicolai Manuscript from the monastery of St. Mark in Florence reflects Byzantine practice from the third to the eighth centuries. The following is omitted from the rite of ordination of a deaconess: "Lord our God, in your providence you send the working and abundance of your Holy Spirit on those who through your inscrutable power are constituted liturgical ministers to serve your immaculate mysteries." John Morinus, *Commentarius de Sacris Ecclesiae Ordinationibus* (Antwerp: Kalverstraat, 1695): 55–57, trans. John Wijnggaards at www.womenpriests.org/traditio/deac_gr1.htm.

[119]"I commend to you our sister Phoebe, a deaconess of the Church at Cenchreae, that you may receive her in the Lord as befits the saints, and help her in whatever she may require from you, for she has been a helper of many and of myself as well" (Rom. 16:1–2).

bility that the word "deacon" was gender-inclusive (and therefore "deaconess" was less used), arguments still exist that those who followed Phoebe, as the office of deacon developed, were not deacons at all but belonged to a "fourth order" of service neither identical nor equal to the male diaconate. This "fourth order," the supposition continues, in turn did not incur or imply ordination as it is now or was then understood.[120] Yet, the same bishops pronounced the same words, and imposed hands on the heads of male and female deacons alike. It is most clear in the affirmative that the negative argument is neither well done nor evenhanded, and it has grown only in proportion to the revival of scholarship that discovered historical facts that support the concept of an ordained female diaconate. It is unfortunate that the history of ordained women deacons in the Church causes some to attempt to either disprove or at least disregard it.[121]

Historical disputations notwithstanding, the clearest point that may be understood by the conflict between the differing factions is that, independent of the developing notions of sacramental ordination, however men were determined to be deacons in the ancient Church, so too were women identically determined, and their service and representation of the body of Christ was identically ceremonially conferred. We will return to this later. In fact, strenuous argumentation against the historical ordination of women deacons argues as well against the ordination of men deacons.

---

[120]Laurence Rand, "Ordination of Women to the Diaconate," *Communio* 8 (Winter 1981): 370–83. Also, from November 29 to December 4, 1999, the International Theological Commission, which is headed by Joseph Cardinal Ratzinger, met to consider an eighteen-page working document that apparently presents this concept. The document was prepared by one of twenty-nine priests on the thirty-member Commission, Henrique de Noronha Galvào (1937–), whose major scholarship appears as *Die existentielle Gotteserkenntnis bei Augustin: eine hermeneutische Lektüure der Confessiones* (Einsiedeln: Johannes, 1981), originally presented as the author's doctoral thesis at Universität Regensburg, 1979.

[121]The premier effort in this regard is Aimé Georges Martimort, *Les diaconesses: Essai historique* (1982); in English: Aimé Georges Martimort, *Deaconesses: An Historical Study*, trans. K. D. Whitehead (San Francisco: Ignatius Press, 1986).

The female diaconate of history was not a separate, less equal, order of deaconess.

What women deacons of history did is what they have always done and do today, independent of any argument as to whether they were sacramentally ordained (or even as to whether they can be so ordained now). Women eventually came to be included in the roster of clerics in some sees, an indication of the relationship the diocesan bishop believed he had with them, equally independent of any definition of their precise canonical status the present can superimpose upon the past. Routinely, women deacons handled the religious affairs of other women, prepared them for sacraments (especially for baptism), and baptized other women as well.

There are sufficient documents to support the historical fact of women deacons, many of which are delineated in the following chapter. What ordination meant at the time of these documents, compared with the present theology of ordination and orders, could be cause for concern except that it is clear that the early Church found the ministry of women to women an absolute necessity. In any event, the fact (or nonfact) of sacramental ordination of women at the time women served as deacons (or deaconesses) in the early Church in and of itself neither proves nor disproves the possibility of sacramental ordination of women to the diaconate today. The ordained service of women (whatever that meant) was judged necessary and proper to the early Church, and so the ordained service of women (whatever that might become) is arguably necessary and proper today, given the numbers of women preparing for and serving in ministry.

Even if the precise history of women deacons may be clouded, it would appear that bishops routinely formalized the service of women in the Church independent of whatever personal commitments — to marriage or to monastery — the women may have made for themselves. This formalization was referred to as ordination sufficiently enough to present a convincing argument that however the ordination of male deacons was considered in the early Church, so was the ordination of women deacons equally

considered. That is, those orders that were conferred were conferred equally. In any event, the matter of the sacrament of orders
was increasingly understood as, and agreed upon as, the imposition
of hands, not the person receiving the sacrament.[122]

A more pertinent question might be whether the development
of the theology of orders progressed from understandings of the
episcopacy, presbyterate, and diaconate (to which women were
admitted) or from understandings of four separate orders: bishop,
priest, deacon, and deaconess. Even if the latter is chosen (or
determined) the fact remains that deaconess (as distinct from deacon) was, and can therefore remain as, part of the sacrament of
orders.

To consider deaconesses as distinct from deacons would change
the request from inclusion of women in the grade of the restored
permanent diaconate to the revival of the ancient order of deaconess. The problem that could arise would be the determination
by Church authority that such revival of the role and status of deaconess would require installation, not ordination. With installed
deaconesses, rather than ordained women deacons, the question
of participation in the clergy and ordinary ability to participate in
sacramental power and juridical authority would arise. For example, acolytes and lectors are installed, and are not clerics; neither
would installed deaconesses be clerics. Nonclerical installed deaconesses would not be part of the bishop's household, but simply
members of the laity ineligible for any claim to support, however that might be determined. They would also be ineligible, in
the usual course of events, for ordinary sacramental faculties or
juridical authority requiring clerical status. Nonclerical installed
deaconesses would merely form yet another distinction among
women who might be able to be granted extraordinary faculties
(for baptism and witnessing marriage) perhaps even routinely because of a given bishop's stated need.[123] But they would not be

---

[122]Joseph Martos, *Doors to the Sacred* (Garden City, N.Y.: Doubleday, 1981), 481.

[123]Regarding the delegation of the authority to witness marriages to a lay minister,
"The diocesan bishop may concede this delegation only in cases where there are no priests
or deacons available and after he shall have obtained for his own diocese a favorable *votum*

deacons. This would not advance the status of women in the Church. Whether women are to be admitted to the diaconate as deacons or as deaconesses, they ought to be admitted through ordination, and therefore be made clerics in the ordinary manner.

Ordination of women to the permanent diaconate would require a partial derogation from Canon 1024.

It is not appropriate to conflate all possibilities or all grades of orders into the single proscription of Canon 1024 ("Only a baptized male validly receives sacred ordination"), but only to consider them separately.[124] That is, the proscriptions against the ordination as bishop, priest, or deacon. The question of the permanent diaconate must be considered separately. Neither is it helpful to digress at this point relative to the improbability of the ability of law to definitively determine the validity (as opposed to the legitimacy) of a sacrament. The presumption of Canon 1024 is that the Church cannot validly ordain a woman because it cannot legitimately ordain a woman. It is clear that the restrictions of Canon 1024 are intended as restrictions of legitimacy extended to restrictions of validity, but the doctrinal implications are restricted to episcopacy and priesthood. The confusion of legitimacy and validity, and the conflation of the three levels or grades of orders to which Canon 1024 applies (diaconate, presbyterate, episcopacy), together seem at first to eliminate any possibility of the Church's returning to its tradition of women deacons.

But the point of Canon 1024 (Canon 968 in the 1917 Code) is to exclude women from the sacrifice of the altar, not from ordination to ministry. Again, since Church authority has appar-

---

from the conference of bishops and the necessary permission from the Holy See." "Some Questions Regarding Collaboration of Non-Ordained Faithful in Priests' Sacred Ministry," co-signed by the prefects of the Congregations for Clergy, Doctrine of the Faith, Divine Worship and Discipline of the Sacraments, Bishops, Evangelization of Peoples, Institutes of Consecrated Life and Societies of Apostolic Life, and the presidents of the Councils for the Laity and Interpretation of Legislative Texts, *Origins* 27, no. 24 (November 27, 1997): 406.

[124]Canon 1024: "Sacram ordinationem valide recipit solus vir baptizatus." It is well to recall that the language has changed as the arguments for women's ordination grew louder. Formerly, it was more usual to "consecrate" bishops.

ently ruled out discussion on the possibility of women priests or bishops, and the Congregation for the Doctrine of the Faith has determined that the most recent papal document on the matter belongs irrevocably to the deposit of faith, a derogation from the law would not endanger these determinations. Derogation from the law to allow the restoration of the female diaconate as an or-dained ministry, equal to the male diaconate, would not change any doctrinal understandings of the Church.

The whole Church calls forth both women and men to ministry.

The equal ministry of service is performed by equal persons. The equality of persons is a philosophical given. The ultimate question in this discussion, then, is whether theological principles are built on philosophical principles. Again the question: Is grace built on nature?

In considering the possibility of the call of women to ordained ministry as deacons, the question arises how the proper under-standing of maleness and femaleness extends to Roman Catholic ecclesiology and, ultimately, to the diaconate. There are familiar distinctions of the Church: (1) the Church as the mystery and sacrament of salvation; (2) the Church as the fullness of Christ and of fellowship; (3) the Church as the Body of Christ; (4) the Church as the People of God; (5) the Church as a society; (6) the Church and the kingdom.[125] These distinctions help in formu-lating the question of the history of female deacons in the light of *Lumen Gentium*'s definition of the Church: "a visible organiza-tion through which [Christ] communicates truth and grace to all men."[126] *Lumen Gentium* continues, "the society structured with

---

[125]Taken from Karl Rahner, ed., *Encyclopedia of Theology: The Concise Sacramentum Mundi* (New York: Seabury Press, 1975), article on "Church" Part II, "Ecclesiology" by Marie-Joseph le Guillou, 209–21.

[126]It is not useful to beat these locutions to death: obviously, the translator should have just said "all" or "all people." If the Church means "all" or "all people" when it says "men," then past diction is a little less grating. Church authority's writers are careful to use "male" instead of "men" in matters pertaining to ordination; the original intent of noting that only baptized men validly received orders refers as well to "men" as "human beings." Such would be more in the tradition of sacramental theology.

hierarchical organs and the mystical body of Christ, . . . are not to be thought of as two realities." It is the Church that carries on the work of Christ both in the person of Christ, the head of the Church, and in His name, that is, in the name of the Church. The Church's function, in the words of Luke, is "to bring good news to the poor . . . to heal the contrite of heart" (Luke 4:18) and "to seek and to save what was lost" (Luke 19:10).[127]

These are the functions of the whole Church, not its restricted governing class, or even of those living specific ministerial vocations, whether secular or religious, cleric or lay. The economy of the Church, however, encourages specific vocations to be more responsible for some areas of this call to heal and to evangelize, to be in life the living compassion of Jesus the Christ. The Church has also developed a mechanism for noting a specific responsibility for the healing and evangelization of the whole Church, and we know that as ordination. The response to this established mechanism has varied over the centuries, more or less in keeping with the needs and generosity of the People of God. At present, needs are calling forth new expressions of generosity.

It is well here to determine who makes up this Church, this *ecclesia,* which calls women to the diaconate. There is, admittedly, a tension between the modern hierarchical Church as a structure created from administrative and operational necessity, and the function of that hierarchical Church given over to the ministry to and by a community of believers. Every country in every century has held this division in one way or another. Presently, the Catholic Common Ground Initiative in the United States is designed to create space to discuss a wide diversity of matters typically at issue between the "liberal" and the "conservative"[128] wings of the

---

[127]*Lumen Gentium,* no. 8, in *Vatican Council II: The Conciliar and Post Conciliar Documents,* ed. Austin Flannery, O.P. (Wilmington, Del.: Scholarly Resources, 1975), 357.

[128]These divisions are not meaningful for many Catholics, especially those who came of age after Vatican II. More "liberal" organizations would include Call to Action, Celibacy Is The Issue, Corps of Reserve Priests United in Service (CORPUS), Association for Rights of Catholics in the Church, FutureChurch, Women's Ordination Conference, Catholics Speak Out, National Coalition of American Nuns, Inclusive Church, and Coalition of Concerned Catholics. More "conservative" organizations would include Catholic Educa-

Church. In announcing the Catholic Common Ground Initiative, Joseph Cardinal Bernardin noted specifically that

> an increasing polarization within the Church and, at times, a meanspiritedness have hindered the kind of dialogue that helps us address our mission and concerns. As a result, the unity of the Church is threatened, the great gift of the Second Vatican Council is in danger of being seriously undermined, the faithful members of the Church are weary, and our witness to government, society, culture is compromised.[129]

The initial question of the Catholic Common Ground Initiative is "Will the Catholic Church in the United States enter the new millennium as a church of promise augmented by the faith of rising generations and able to be a leavening force in our culture?"[130] While several issues (including the role of women, religious education, Church teachings on sexuality, formation of lay ministers, questions of authority, collegiality, and subsidiarity, and the survival and missions of Catholic schools, health care, and social service agencies) are noted as potential for dialogue, the basic call is for dialogue itself. Regular public discussions between and among persons representing differing sides of various questions are held nationwide.

The discussions have not specifically focused on ordaining women deacons, which topic may be obscured by these and by other recent discussions in lay ministry. There has, in fact, been a great deal of recent discussion on the development of a specific "lay ministry" within the Church, including the concept of "ordained" lay ministers, who would be members of a pastoral team that would include *viri probati* priests — lay men not necessarily traditionally trained or formed.[131] This is important in the current

---

tion Network, The National Association of Catholic Home Educators, Catholics United for Life, Faith Movement, Knights of Columbus, and the Latin Liturgy Association.

[129]Joseph Cardinal Bernardin, statement at Catholic Common Ground News Conference, August 12, 1996.

[130]"Called to Be Catholic" (New York: National Pastoral Life Center, 1996).

[131]See F. Lobinger, *Like His Brothers and Sisters: Ordaining Community Leaders* (Quezon City, Philippines: Claretian Publications, 1998).

climate and the present discussion, as we recall that presently all women are laity. Hence we must examine the realm of lay ministry if we wish to understand the present ministerial function of women in the Church, functions and service that presage a need for more formal incorporation of women's service through orders.[132]

Women called forth to ministry must belong to the juridical society of the Church.

The question becomes: how exactly can women fit into both the structure and the function of the Church? How have women been called; how are women now called to serve? We could look at certain women of the Church — Catherine of Siena, or Teresa of Avila, or Joan of Arc, or Mother Teresa, or even Dorothy Day — and argue that women always have been and continue to be the very center of the very structure and function of the Church. Despite their unrepresentative membership in the calendar of saints, even in modern times,[133] women saints are well known in the Church. However, one does well to argue the reverse, and present the historical probability that women have been at the Church's periphery, both structurally and functionally, throughout history. The central question is how one views "Church."

Of necessity, the "Church" considered here is the hierarchically ministerial Church, not the entire People of God. This "Church-as-structure," a hierarchical and juridical society, symbolizes the functions of the various people of the Church and is organized along the lines referred to earlier: bishops, priests, deacons. "Church-as-structure" is not identical to what the Second Vati-

---

[132]"In the Church there is a diversity of ministry but unity of mission. To the apostles and their successors Christ has entrusted the office of teaching, sanctifying and governing in his name and by his power. But the laity are made to share in the priestly, prophetical and kingly office of Christ; they have therefore, in the Church and in the world, their own assignment in the mission of the whole People of God." Decree on the Apostolate of Lay People, *Apostolicam Actuositatem*, in Flannery, *Vatican Council II*, 768.

[133]"In the first eight decades of the twentieth century, for example, the proportion of canonized saints numbered 75 percent men to 25 percent women." Elizabeth A. Johnson, *Friends of God and Prophets*, 27, citing Pierre Delooz, "The Social Function of the Canonization of Saints," in *Models of Holiness*, Concilium 129, ed. C. Duquoc and C. Floristan (New York: Seabury, 1979), 14–25.

can Council discussed as *communio,* which is the Church's nature and its mystery.[134]

The Church functions through the ministries of the whole People of God: clerics both secular and religious: bishops, priests, deacons; installed lectors and acolytes; religious both clerical and lay; the secular laity,[135] those vowed in secular institutes, and those who live as consecrated virgins or hermits.[136]

When we specifically extricate women from this great crowd, there are two questions before us: as regards structure, what can women be? and, as regards function, what can women do? These questions women continue to ask, and the response from an ordinary organizational standpoint is that whereas women were once called to diaconal service, in fact explicitly to the diaconate, so now women are called again. The testimony of history is not conclusive, but it more strongly points to ordination (as opposed to installation) of women deacons. To allow women to function as deacons without integrating women as ordained members of the structure of the Church dilutes both function and structure.

The contemporary Church calls for ordained women deacons.

Official and unofficial Church bodies in various countries have called for the restoration of the female diaconate. Unofficial Church bodies speak in accord with Canon 212, in exercising the right and answering the obligation of the laity to "make known their needs, especially spiritual ones, and their desires to the pastors of the Church."[137] For example, in October 1998, the majority

---

[134]"*Communio* is not a description of the church's structure. It describes its nature or, as the council puts it, its 'mystery.'" Walter Kasper, *Theology and Church* (New York: Crossroad, 1989), 151.

[135]As noted earlier, *Lumen Gentium,* nos. 31 and 43 seem contradictory relative to the ways in which individuals fit into the juridical structure of the Church. While religious are both clerical and lay, "the laity" by and large refers to the secular laity not otherwise incorporated into any society of apostolic life.

[136]Eremitic life is deep within the tradition of the Church, and it is from the hermitage that many competent spiritual directors emerge. The life is treated legally in Canon 603. "The Order of Virgins; hermits and widows" are discussed in *Vita Consecrata,* no. 7.

[137]Canon 212.2. Also, "In accord with the knowledge, competence and preeminence which they possess, they have the right and even at times the duty to manifest to the

of 276 delegates to "Dialogue for Austria," convened by "Wir sind Kirche" ("We are the Church") voted "in support of the establishment of a steady [stabile] diaconate for women and ask the bishops to steadfastly support this in Rome, even if it should be made possible only for parts of the Church."[138] Wir sind Kirche, established in Austria in 1995 in response to the scandal surrounding the former Archbishop of Vienna, Hans Hermann Cardinal Groer, has the support of all but one conservative Austrian bishop. Wir sind Kirche does not call for the ordination of women to priesthood.[139]

Official Church bodies have asked for the ordination of women deacons as well. The German bishops, and most recently Bishop Karl Lehmann, Bishop of Mainz and head of the Bishops' conference, have called for the reestablishment of the female diaconate.[140] The German bishops called for women deacons as early as 1971, and again in 1975.[141] An international gathering

---

sacred pastors their opinion on matters which pertain to the good of the Church, and they have a right to make their opinion known to the other Christian faithful, with due regard for the integrity of faith and morals and reverence toward their pastors, and with consideration for the common good and the dignity of persons" (Canon 212.3).

[138]John L. Allen Jr., "A Dramatic Step toward Reform," *National Catholic Reporter,* November 6, 1998, 3–5. Votes in favor: 212. "Themes of the Dialogue," trans. Hubert Feichtlbauer, 5. Christoph Cardinal Schonborn, Archbishop of Vienna, said in response that as far as women deacons were concerned, he was "not sure what God's will is yet." Pope John Paul II ignored the results and warned against democratization. John L. Allen Jr., "Krenn at the Center of Austrian Strife," *National Catholic Reporter* 35, no. 8 (December 18, 1998): 6.

[139]There were five hundred thousand signatures on the petition. Baryli Waltraud, "L'Église autrichienne souhaite le départ d'un évêque ultra-conservateur," *Le Monde*, December 28, 1998. "Ce dialogue pour l'Autriche, entre 276 délégués triés sur le volet et des représentants de la conférence épiscopale, a eu lieu fin octobre à Salzbourg. Les revendications portaient sur une plus grande transparence dans les nominations, sur l'ordination de femmes diacres et l'accès au sacerdoce d'hommes mariés pour remédier à la pénurie de prêtres." This article discusses the resistance of one Austrian Bishop, Kurt Krenn, to Wir sind Kirche.

[140]"Bischof Lehmann wirbt für das Diakonat der Frau," *Frankfurter Allgemeine Zeitung* (October 7, 1996): 4. Bishop Lehmann was Karl Rahner's assistant in Rome and in Munich, and later collaborated with Hans Urs von Balthasar on the founding of the theological journal *Communio*. Werner Loser, "Karl Rahner and Hans Urs von Balthasar (Theologians Discussed by Werner Loser)," interview by Brian W. Hughes, *America* 181, no. 11 (October 16, 1999): 16.

[141]The Joint Synod of the Dioceses of the Federal Republic of Germany asked Paul VI "to permit the ordination of women to the diaconate." *Gemeinsame Synode der Bistümer in der Bundesrepublik Deutschland, Offizielle Gesamtausgabe I* (Freiburg: Herder, 1976), 634, *votum* 7.1,3 (as cited in Canon Law Society of America, *The Canonical Implications of*

of theologians met at a meeting hosted by the Academy of the Rottenburg-Stuttgart Diocese in April 1997 and asked the German Bishops to request an indult from the Vatican to ordain women to the diaconate.[142]

In the United States, a committee of the Canon Law Society of America prepared a study, published as *The Canonical Implications of Ordaining Women to the Permanent Diaconate*, which found that women have been ordained deacons in the past and can be so ordained again in individual local circumstances depending on cultural factors.

> The committee has reached the conclusion that, in light of its research, ordination of women to the permanent diaconate is possible, and may even be desirable for the United States in the present cultural circumstances.[143]

This conclusion is echoed in many quarters. In the United States, as elsewhere, journals present the diaconate for women as a clear possibility:

> The restoration of the diaconate for women, which is rooted in Scripture and does not contradict the logic of *Ordinatio Sacerdotalis*, may be a first step in responding to the call of women, while at the same time fulfilling a great pastoral need.[144]

The serious research of many scholars and scholarly groups, as well as the widespread calls for women to be ordained to the diaconate, ·

Ordaining Women to the Permanent Diaconate [Washington, D.C.: Canon Law Society of America, 1995], 4).

[142]"German bishops' conference spokesman Rudolf Hammerschmidt said 'a number of our members' support seeking an indult to permit the ordination of women to the diaconate in Germany, but 'it is still under consideration.'" "Conference Calls for Indult," *National Catholic Reporter* 33, no. 26 (May 2, 1997): 9.

[143]Canon Law Society of America, *The Canonical Implications of Ordaining Women to the Permanent Diaconate*, 1–2. The document was not formally adopted by the Society, but Resolution 5 to receive and publish the report carried with a voice vote, three abstentions. *Proceedings of the 57th Annual Convention Montreal, Que., October 16–19, 1995* (Washington, D.C.: Canon Law Society of America, 1995), 495. The document was received, published, and passed to various professional, academic, and theological groups and societies for comment.

[144]Unsigned editorial, "Women in the Church," *America* 181, no. 17 (November 27, 1999): 3.

requires the most positive interpretation possible be given to the great body of historical evidence that women, who indeed were called to and served in diaconal roles, in fact were ordained to the diaconate, and so can be ordained again.

Summary

While liturgical restrictions may have clouded the role of women deacons, the female diaconate of history was not a separate, less equal, order of deaconess. Ordination of women to the diaconate would require a partial derogation from Canon 1024. The whole Church calls forth both men and women to ministry. Women called forth to ministry must belong to the juridical society of the Church. The contemporary Church calls for ordained women deacons. Therefore, women are and have been called to the diaconate.

V. There are stronger arguments from scripture, history, tradition, and theology that women may be ordained deacons than that women may not be ordained deacons.

The prior arguments from tradition and theology are supported by scripture and history.

The historical argument on behalf of women deacons continues and is bound (as it must be) to definitive interpretations of texts. The present argument is a compilation and interpretation of the reliable sources that support the concept. As noted earlier, history alone can neither prove nor disprove the possibility of the Church's ordaining women deacons, but it certainly shows a widely accepted role for women in centuries past, at times a greater role than in the present.

For the most part, the female diaconate appears to have faded along with the male diaconate, in the West around the fifth century and in the East in the ninth century. The liturgical import of male deacons retained the office through the seventh century in the West and, strongly, through the eleventh century in the East, although it never completely died out. The diaconate has been restored in the West.

The fact of an ordained female diaconate in history is supported by two points: (1) the word "deacon" could have been, and probably was, gender inclusive, and so the ample evidence of the diaconate in both the East and the West may include women, even where the word "deaconess" is not used; (2) the principle of subsidiarity existed in the Church's first thousand years, and so local practices of ordaining women to the diaconate might well have continued long after the female diaconate appears to have faded.[145]

---

[145]Ute Eisen analyzes eighteen examples of epigraphs on tombs of women deacons: two from Palestine (fourth and seventh centuries), five from Asia Minor (second, fourth, and fifth centuries), three from Greece (fourth century), five from Macedonia (fourth, fifth, and sixth centuries) and three from the West (possibly second, fifth, and certainly sixth centuries). See Ute E. Eisen, *Women Officeholders in Early Christianity: Epigraphical and Literary Studies*, trans. Linda M. Maloney (Collegeville, Minn.: Liturgical Press, 2000), 158–98. Originally published as *Amtsträgerinnen im frühen Christentum: Epigraphische und literarische Studien* (Göttingen: Vandenhoeck & Ruprecht, 1996). For literary evidence of

By viewing the chronology of East and West simultaneously, the evolution of the juridical and the ministerial functions of women can be more easily traced.

The preeminent historical testimony regarding female deacons comes in scripture. While the women of scripture who served, like Phoebe, as *diaconos* of the Church at Cenchreae could not be considered deacons of today (that is, within a juridical structure as such), their ministries in many respects mirrored the ministries of men deacons, whose descendants are among those in the diaconate as reconstituted after Vatican II. Obviously, the present formal structure of the Church, enabled as it is by modern communications, cannot be projected retroactively upon the Church as it was forming. Facts and trends in one local Church may not have applied to or continued in another local Church.

The two New Testament passages that specifically refer to deaconesses, Romans 16:1–2 and 1 Timothy 3:11, are clear enough: "I commend you to our sister Phoebe, deaconess of the Church at Cenchreae"[146] and "... deacons must be respectable men whose word can be trusted.... In the same way, the women must be respectable, not gossips but sober and quite reliable."[147]

It is clear that in Romans Phoebe is not being given an honorary title, but that she exists as a minister to the Church at Cenchreae; the passage suggests not that she be subordinated, but that she be deferred to.[148] Scholarship continues on the references to "the women" to whom Paul refers, either by name (Phoebe) or as unnamed ministers in his letter to Timothy, but one careful

---

the diaconate's inclusion of women, Eisen depends on Gryson and Martimort, as well as on Marie-Josèphe Aubert, *Des femmes diacres: Un nouveau chemin pour l'Église*, preface by Régine Pernoud (Paris: Beauchesne, 1987), and Dirk Ansorge, "Der Diakonat der Frau: Zum gegenwärtigen Forschungsstand," in *Liturgie und Frauenfrage: Ein Beitrag zur Frauenforschung aus liturgiewissenschaftlicher Sicht*, ed. Teresa Berger and Albert Gerhards (St. Ottilien: EOS Verlag, 1990), 31–65, among others.

[146]Romans 16:1. Some commentators believe Phoebe was the bearer of the epistle to the Romans.

[147]1 Timothy 3:8, 11. The construction requires women deacons, not the wives of deacons, to make sense.

[148]J. Massyngberde Ford, "Biblical Material Relevant to the Ordination of Women," *Journal of Ecumenical Studies* 10 (Fall 1973): 669–94, 676.

linguistic delineation of the text, by Jennifer H. Stiefel, finds that "the evidence in 1 Timothy 3.11 for diaconal ministry of women is strong."[149] While not conclusive regarding the actual status of women deacons, 1 Timothy points to a deep understanding of the early Church about the possibilities of women ministering in an official and coordinated capacity within the Church. Stiefel concludes:

> Had Paul neglected to mention either her name or her role, we should not have known of Phoebe, [deaconess] of Cenchreae. Had they not been slaves and thus available for torture, Pliny would not have commented on the two women *ministrae* (probably [deaconesses]) of the Christians he was investigating.... Here as elsewhere it is clear that later conceptions of what is possible or appropriate have largely ruled, and still influence, the interpretation of the role of women in the early Church. The challenge to every interpreter is to respond beyond one's own boundaries to the intimations of the text.[150]

K. K. FitzGerald notes that this particular passage is commented upon by Origen and presents his commentary:

> This text teaches with the authority of the Apostle that even women are instituted deacons in the Church. This was the function which was exercised in the Church at Cenchreae by Phoebe, who was the object of high praise and recommendation by Paul.... And thus this text teaches at the same time two things: that there are, as we have already said, women deacons in the Church, and that women, who have given assistance to so many people and who by their good works deserve to be praised by the Apostle, ought to be accepted in the diaconate.[151]

FitzGerald continues to note other commentaries that affirm the understanding of Phoebe and the women of 1 Timothy as true

---

[149]Jennifer H. Stiefel, "Women Deacons in 1 Timothy: A Linguistic and Literary Look at 'Women Likewise...' (1 Tim. 3.11)," *New Testament Studies,* 41 (1995): 442–57, 456.

[150]Stiefel, "Women Deacons in 1 Timothy," 457. "Deaconess" and "deaconesses" in brackets replace Stiefel's use of the Greek.

[151]*Commentary on Romans 10:17,* as quoted by Kyriaki Karidoyanes FitzGerald, "The Characteristics and Nature of the Order of Deaconess" in *Women and the Priesthood,* ed. Thomas Hopko (Crestwood, N.Y.: St. Vladimir's Seminary Press, 1983), 77.

women deacons of the Church: "[Paul] is speaking of those who hold the rank of Deaconess.... For that order is necessary and useful and honorable in the Church."[152]

As J. M. Ford points out, additional New Testament support can be found in Acts 6:1–6, which uses only the verb *diakonein* (not the male *diakonos*), mirroring the service of Martha in Luke 10:38–42 (Martha and Mary). In Acts, those chosen at that time receive the imposition of hands, but the naming of seven men ought not eliminate the possibility of women being included among the disciples in general or among those called to serve in particular. The word *diakonein* refers not only to the service of the seven men, but also to Martha's service in Luke.[153] Further, the ministry of the women who accompanied Jesus in his public ministry can be seen as diaconal. Just as the apostles are now seen as analogous to bishops, so ought the women who accompanied Jesus be now understood as deaconesses.[154] In fact, there are multiple examples of women disciples in the Gospels: tradition has accepted that women were among the seventy (or seventy-two) disciples (Luke 10:1–12); it is a woman who bears witness to Jesus in John 4:39; the women who followed Jesus are acknowledged repeatedly (Luke 23:49); and some have argued that Mary had the dual role of mother and disciple, noting that Cana comes directly after the calling of the disciples (John 1:35–51) and that once Jesus showed himself at Cana, his mother and other relatives and disciples accompanied him (John 2:11).[155]

The understanding of the terms "deacon" and "deaconess" must not be argued out of context. They meant what they meant in the early Church, and they mean what they mean (or could mean) today, given the present understanding of sacramental theology. Historical exegesis can and does argue strongly that women served

---

[152] *Homily 11 on Timothy* as quoted by K. K. FitzGerald, "Order of Deaconess" in *Women and the Priesthood*, 78.

[153] J. M. Ford, "Biblical Material Relevant to the Ordination of Women," 671.

[154] Ibid., 672. Ford refers to Hans Conzelmann, *The Theology of Luke* (1960) 46ff., in his explication of Luke 8:1–3 and Luke 10:38–42.

[155] J. M. Ford, "Biblical Material Relevant to the Ordination of Women," 673–74.

in the capacity of deaconess, and (as we will come to later) were ordained with contemporary ceremonies identical to those of men well into the fourth century in the West and into the ninth century in the East. That is, whatever ordination meant at the time, it was granted equally to men and to women deacons.

The writer of the Canon Law Society of America 1995 report on women deacons argues, along with Roger Gryson and Aimé Georges Martimort, that to call Phoebe deaconess with its current reading is anachronistic "since this term [deaconess] was utilized to specify an ecclesiastical institution of a much later date,"[156] but does not argue the same limitation to men. If the diaconate is an ecclesiastical institution, and not one normatively instituted by Christ to include only men, then there is no reason to exclude women. If, as the writer states, it is at this time that the original charism is on its way to becoming an office, there is no need to argue for anything beyond that fact. That is, the original charism of *diakonia* in the Church, as a ministry of all the baptized, was on its way to become a stable office of the Church centuries hence. What could have been posited, and what might be posited should Church authority, when it takes up the matter, definitively find that women will not be admitted to the diaconate, is the possibility that there were four ordained orders: bishop, priest, deacon, deaconess. A further finding might present that since deaconess did not survive to the present understanding of ordination, it remains an installed or appointed rank, which would only be anachronistically called "deaconess" in equation with "deacon." (This would place the order of deaconess as a minor order, along with the former minor orders of subdeacon, lector, acolyte, porter, and exorcist. It would not account for the Church's never before

---

[156]*The Canonical Implications of Ordaining Women to the Permanent Diaconate*, Report of an Ad Hoc Committee of the Canon Law Society of America (Washington, D.C.: Canon Law Society of America, 1995), 8, citing Roger Gryson, *The Ministry of Women in the Early Church*, trans. Jean Laporte and Mary Louise Hall (Collegeville, Minn.: Liturgical Press, 1976), 3–4; Aimé Georges Martimort, *Deaconesses: An Historical Study*, trans. K. D. Whitehead (San Francisco: Ignatius Press, 1986), 22; and A. Kalsbach, s.v. "Diaconisse," *Reallexikon für Antike und Christentum*, III, ed. Theodor Klauser (Stuttgart: Anton Hiersemann, 1957), col. 917.

cleaving the diaconate — half ordained and half not ordained — in this fashion.)

One scholar, Norbert Brockman, posits that the usage ("deaconess") is "clearly in the technical sense of a specific order or office in the priesthood."[157] Such inclusion is not contradictory: the deacon serves the bishop, as does the priest. While the priest can perform the duties of deacon, the deacon cannot perform the duties of priest. Inclusion does not automatically imply expansion. There are clear indications, ceremonially and otherwise, that women ordained deaconesses would not be admitted to priesthood or the episcopacy. Again, there is no contradiction to the concept of orders. As noted earlier, not all who are ordained deacons are eligible to become priests, and not all who are ordained priests are eligible to become bishops. Nothing in scripture or history suggests that the resumed ordination of women to the diaconate would presume that women could be priests, past or present.

Even in light of scripture, tradition, and theology, the interpretation of historical evidence has been challenged.

In fact, historical evidence relative to the female diaconate is incontrovertible except in its interpretation relative to the actual sacramental ordination of women deacons. The two major modern studies, *Le ministère des femmes dans l'Église ancienne* (1972) (*The Ministry of Women in the Early Church*, 1976) by Roger Gryson and *Les diaconesses: Essai historique* (1982) (*Deaconesses: An Historical Study*, 1986) by Aimé Georges Martimort, disagree in many points and in fact form a fairly complete open debate on historical evidence and interpretations. Gryson's book, published first, argues toward the possibilities for ordaining women; Martimort's rejoinder argues against any interpretation that women were ordained.[158] Gryson presents historical evidence that seems to give

---

[157]Norbert Brockman, *Ordained to Service: A Theology of the Permanent Diaconate* (Hicksville, N.Y.: Exposition Press, 1976), 4.

[158]Martimort responded to Gryson's 1972 book with Aimé Georges Martimort, "A propos des ministères féminins dans l'Église," *Bulletin de Littérature Ecclésiastique* 74, 103–8; Gryson responded in later editions of *Le ministère des femmes dans L'Église ancienne*; Martimort then published *Les Diaconesses: Essai historique* (1982).

a sacramental character to the undisputed ordination of women, which Martimort denies. In fact, Martimort argues against the possibility of any inferences about the ordination of women from the *Apostolic Constitutions,* a position Gryson calls "excessive."[159] We will return to these differences of interpretation of fact later.

The female diaconate as present in scripture and tradition reinforces the historical evidence of women deacons.

The female diaconate in the Letters of Paul is without question the descendant of the ministry of the women accompanying Jesus:

> Now after this he made his way through towns and villages preaching, and proclaiming the Good News of the kingdom of God. With him went the Twelve, as well as certain women who had been cured of evil spirits and ailments; Mary surnamed the Magdalene, from whom seven demons had gone out, Joanna the wife of Herod's steward Chuza, Susanna, and several others who provided for them out of their own resources. (Luke 8:1–3)

It is not only commonly understood that women served in some official capacity as deaconesses in the early Church, longer in the East than in the West, but, as Norbert Brockman has pointed out, formal sources are complemented by "the liturgy, popular devotion, and art (the iconography of the Eastern Churches, e.g.)."[160] The Orthodox Church commemorates a number of women deacons, among them St. Phoebe (September 3), St. Macrina (July 19), St. Nonna (August 6), St. Melania (December 31), St. Theosebia (January 10), St. Gorgonia (February 23), St. Olympias (July 25), St. Apollonia (February 9), and St. Xenia (January 24). All were known as deaconesses in the early Church; some were foundresses of great monasteries, others were teachers, mothers, or wives of male saints. However, their ordination is not questioned. For example:

> St. Xenia (January 24) was the only daughter of a Constantinopolitan senator of the fifth century. In order to avoid a forced

---

[159]Gryson, *The Ministry of Women in the Early Church,* 120.
[160]Brockman, *Ordained to Service,* xi.

marriage, she fled to Cyprus with two of her maid-servants. She was then sent to Alexandria by St. Epiphanius, where she was ordained a deaconess by Patriarch Theophilus. Later, St. Xenia founded a monastery named after St. Stephen the Deacon and Protomartyr. She was often consulted as a "spiritual mother" by many people in the towns near the monastery.[161]

Both the Latin, or Western, and the Eastern Churches hold epigraphical evidence about these women deacons known through literary evidence. Inscriptions from Palestine and its vicinity, from Asia Minor, Greece, Macedonia, and the West (Gaul, Italy, and Dalmatia) present ample evidence of the existence of women deacons.[162] For example, an inscription in Cappadocia:

> Here lies the deacon Maria of pious and blessed memory, who according to the words of the apostle raised children, sheltered guests, washed the feet of the saints, and shared her bread with the needy. Remember her, Lord, when she comes into your kingdom.[163]

The early Church evidenced women deacons.

By the first century, the Church was distinguishing between sacramental and nonsacramental functions and tasks and also distinguishing between personal charisms and the subordination of all charisms to the mission of the Church. This traditional view of sacrament and its concomitant promise of the efficacy of a sacrament (as a ministry of the Church) independent of the minister (insofar as the minister is acting with and for the whole Church) is an initial indication that women, where they acted for the Church, were regarded as ministers of the Church. Further, insofar as their actions were part of the sacramental ministry of the Church, so

---

[161]K. K. FitzGerald, "The Characteristics and Nature of the Order of Deaconess" in *Women and the Priesthood*, ed. Hopko, 78–80. FitzGerald here cites Elisabeth Behr-Sigel, "The Meaning of the Participation of Women in the Life of the Church," *Orthodox Women: Their Role and Participation in the Orthodox Church*, ed. Constance Tarasar and Irina Kirillova (Geneva: World Council of Churches, 1977), 17–29.

[162]See Eisen, *Women Officeholders in Early Christianity*, 158–98.

[163]Ibid., 165.

were they separated out (by sacrament) into a ministering class able to act for and by the Church.

In the *Didascalia Apostolorum,* a second-century Eastern document virtually unknown in modern times before the middle of the nineteenth century,[164] the well-delineated duties of the deaconess — and of the deacon — first appear. The "workers of righteousness" the bishop is told to appoint include both men and women:

> Those that please thee out of all the people thou shalt choose and appoint as deacons: a man for the performance of most things that are required, but a woman for the ministry of women. For there are houses whither thou canst not send a deacon to the women, on account of the heathen, but mayest send a deaconess. Also, because in many other matters the office of a woman deacon is required.[165]

The works the deaconess is to perform include assisting at baptism (including anointing), instructing the newly baptized, visiting the sick: "let a woman rather be devoted to the ministry of women, and a male deacon to the ministry of men."[166] Her ministry comprises the educative and charitable works of the Church, which, where necessary, include both preparation for and the celebration of sacraments.

The description of the ministry of the woman deacon is expanded upon in later documents, for she "has both to keep the door by which women enter the Church and to arrange their places therein. She is the servant of the bishop and no woman may have communication with him except through her."[167] Further,

---

[164]"The *Didascalia of the Apostles* has only been known since 1854.... In ancient times, however, the document enjoyed a rather wide diffusion.... the original *Didascalia* was, however, reworked and, with many revisions and additions, completely incorporated into the great compilation known as the *Apostolic Constitutions."* Martimort, *Deaconesses,* p. 35. The *Didascalia* was probably not put into final form until the third or possibly the fourth century.

[165]"On the appointment of Deacons and Deaconesses," chapter 16 (iii.12–13), *Didascalia Apostolorum,* trans. R. H. Connolly (Oxford: Clarendon Press, 1929), 146–48, 146.

[166]Ibid., 148.

[167]J. G. Davies, "Deacons, Deaconesses and the Minor Orders in the Patristic Period," *Journal of Ecclesiastical History* 14 (1963): 1–15, 3. Davies cites *Didasc.* iii.12–13, reproduced

the female deacon, and not the male deacon, takes the reserved sacrament to sick women.[168]

The admission of women to the order of widows is equally delineated in the *Didascalia,* and it is evident that these were separate and distinct orders of the Church, that of women deacons apparently sacramentally and juridically equal to men deacons, and that of widows subject to the deacons.[169] It is important to recognize the distinct ministries of widows and deaconesses at this early juncture, and especially the fact that widows, unlike deaconesses, were not ordained. Further, widows were generally not admitted to the order of widows until they were at least fifty years of age and presumably no longer interested in marriage. The *Didascalia* distinguishes widows of means and those who were poor, and enjoins the bishop to provide for those widows — young and old — in need. The poverty of both was a charge of the bishop, and he was enjoined to send them meals. The young widows, especially, were a concern, for their poverty might cause them to seek a second marriage. A second marriage was to be guarded against, for the widow would then have belonged to two men.[170] In any event, the order of widows seems to be an appointed state to which widows of means were received in order to assist the bishop in providing for widows of less means.

Some might argue that because the diaconate did not develop uniformly, evidence of women deacons is not normative. There

---

in *Const. Ap.* ii.57; viii.28; Pseudo-Ignatius, *Ad Antioch.,* xii; *Eth. Didasc.,* ii 57, 58 and *Const. Ap.* ii.26.

[168]J. G. Davies, "Deacons, Deaconesses and the Minor Orders," 3, citing *Test. Dom.,* ii. 20.

[169]"On the time for the appointment of Widows," chapter 14 (iii.1–iii.9) *Didascalia Apostolorum,* trans. R. H. Connolly, 130–45. "Ici pourtant il y aurait plutôt lieu d'admettre entre diaconesses et veuves une distinction, qui se rencontre, elle aussi, et plus fréquemment peut-être, dans les textes anciens: les *Constitutions apostoliques,* III, 8, édit. Funk, t. I, p. 197, proclament que les veuves doivent 'obéir aux évêques, aux prêtres, aux diacres, et de plus aux diaconesses.'" J. Forget, "Diaconesses," *Dictionnaire de Théologie Catholique* (Paris: Letouzey et Ané, 1911), 687. This entry recapitulates the ordination liturgy of women deacons by the bishop, with the assistance of the priests, deacons, and deaconesses, by the imposition of hands, but the widows are not so ordained, citing Funk VIII, 19, 20 (p. 525) and VIII, 24 (p. 529). The widows would be obedient to the four classes of ordained persons: bishops, priests, deacons, and deaconesses.

[170]Gryson, *The Ministry of Women,* 36.

is no direct development in the office of deacon — male or female — in the first three centuries of the Church. Even so, there is early evidence of the beginnings of the later codified tripartite understanding of orders: bishop, priest, deacon. For example, Ignatius writes to the Trallians:

> Correspondingly, everyone must show the deacons respect. They represent Jesus Christ, just as the bishop has the role of the Father, and the presbyters are like God's council and an apostolic band. You cannot have a church without these. I am sure you agree with me in this.[171]

It would be incorrect to equate a past institution with the present, but the roots of the present office of deacon or of the possible present restored office of women deacon cannot be ignored.

Some argue that distinct ministries separate men and women in the order of deacons.

Women deacons of the third and fourth centuries, ordained to their ministry with a formula nearly identical to that used for men,[172] but restricted to ministry to women, could not as the men deacons look forward to the possibility of additional office in the Church, i.e., priesthood or the episcopacy.[173] Martimort contends that because women were not encouraged to move from diaconate to priesthood or episcopacy, their diaconal ordination

---

[171]"Letters of Ignatius: Trallians," *Early Christian Fathers*, ed. C. C. Richardson et al. (Philadelphia: Westminster, 1953), 99.

[172]"Concerning a deaconess, I Bartholomew make this constitution: O bishop, you shall lay hands on her in the presence of the presbytery and of the deacons and deaconesses, and say: Eternal God, Father of our Lord Jesus Christ, creator of man and woman, who filled with the Spirit Miriam and Deborah and Anna and Huldah; who did not disdain that your only begotten Son should be born of a woman; who also in the tent of the testimony and in the temple appointed women to be guardians of your holy gates: now look upon this your servant who is being appointed for the ministry, and give her the Holy Spirit and cleanse her from every defilement of body and spirit so that she may worthily complete the work committed to her, to your glory and the praise of your Christ, through whom [be] glory and worship to you in the Holy Spirit for ever. Amen. "Apostolic Constitutions" in Paul F. Bradshaw, *Ordination Rites of the Ancient Churches of East and West* (New York: Pueblo, 1990), 116. Bradshaw also presents Byzantine, East Syrian, and Georgian rites for deaconesses.

[173]J. G. Davies, "Deacons, Deaconesses and the Minor Orders in the Patristic Period," *Journal of Ecclesiastical History* 14 (1963): 3.

did not have the same force of orders as men. Gryson answers that "since the *Constitutions* strongly reject the idea of the priesthood of women, this rationale is meaningless."[174] It is important to re-call here that, despite popular argument to the contrary,[175] the majority of scholars (especially Roger Gryson, but also and no-tably Evangelos D. Theodorou and Cipriano Vagaggini, among others) agree that women were ordained and ordained in the present understanding of the reception of orders.[176] Martimort's study is almost wholly negative, and he is harsh in his criticism of Vagaggini, who published "L'ordinazione delle diaconesse nella tradizione greca e bizantina" in *Orientalia Christiana Periodica* in 1974. Martimort seeks to dismiss the historical fact of the pre-sentation of the chalice to deaconesses and any other facts that cause consideration of their actual ordination.[177]

Gryson answers Martimort's principal objection thusly:

> It may be useful here to prevent an objection. If you derive from the *Apostolic Constitutions* an argument favoring the sacramen-tality of ordination of deaconesses, why not do the same for subdeacons and readers and conclude that their ordination is also sacramental, since it is considered such in the *Apostolic Constitutions?* The answer is that the testimony of the *Consti-tutions* concerning subdeacons is isolated and contradicted by later eastern tradition, whereas it is confirmed by this tradition for deaconesses. Already the *Epitome of the Apostolic Constitu-*

---

[174]Gryson, *The Ministry of Women,* 119.

[175]For example, M. Permaneder, "Diaconesses," in *Dictionnaire Encyclopédique de la Théologie Catholique:* "De nombreux témoiguages démontrent que cette inauguration des diaconesses était, non pas une ordination, mais une simple bénédiction; tels sont ceux de Tertull., *de Baptism,* c. 17; *Const. apost., lib. III, c.9;* Épiphan., *Haeres.* LXIX no. 2; *Haer.* LXXVIII, no. 223." (Paris: Gaume Frères et J. Duprey, Éditeurs, 1869) 281.

[176]Evangelos Theodorou, "The Ministry of the Deaconess in the Greek Orthodox Church," in *The Deaconess: A Service of Women in the World of Today,* World Council of Churches Studies 4 (Geneva: World Council of Churches, 1966), and "Die Weihe, Die Seg-nung der Diakoninnen," *Theologia* 25 (1954): 430–69; Cipriano Vagaggini, "L'ordinazione delle diaconesse nella tradizione grèca e bizantina," *Orientalia Christiana Periodica* 40 (1974): 146–89. Vagaggini (b. 1909), a Benedictine and an expert on liturgy, was a mem-ber of the International Theological Commission. His published paper could comprise much of the suppressed report requested by Paul VI.

[177]As noted earlier, the matter of the sacrament of orders is solely the imposition of hands, and the form is the words.

tions is representative of a tradition, whereas the promotion of the subdiaconate and readers to this same rank is nothing more than a personal opinion of the author and is rejected by tradition. A theological argument, therefore, can be derived in the first case, but not in the second.

Moreover, if we look at the *Constitutions* themselves for traces of a difference of status among the various orders which, because of his own conceptions, would have escaped the systematization which the author achieved, we find that a difference appears, not between the male and female diaconate, contrary to M. Martimort's wishes, but between the female diaconate and the subdiaconate. Actually, from the subdiaconate down, ordination did not present the same degree of solemnity: the text no longer states that it should take place before the presbyters and deacons. This detail is significant. Involuntarily, no doubt, and in spite of his desire to present all ordinations in the same manner, the author reveals the fact that actually the first four ordinations (including the female diaconate) were most solemn celebrations, whereas the following ones (from the subdiaconate down) were far more simple rites.[178]

The above argument from tradition seeks to end any perception that the female deacon was "installed" in a less solemn ceremony, rather than ordained. No matter the overlays of status — deaconess, virgin, widow — there remains clear evidence from tradition that women were solemnly ordained to the diaconate, possibly but not necessarily in concert with their membership in another order, that of widows or virgins.

There is further historical confusion regarding women deacons and widows. While deaconesses and widows are distinct in the first four centuries of the Church, widows could be ordained deaconesses, which might account for confusion in the interpretations of early sources. Therefore, admonitions to "widows" might be

---

[178]Gryson, *The Ministry of Women*, 156. Gryson's text is currently out of print. It would seem to follow, from this analysis and the possibility of derogation from current law, that women may be installed as lectors and acolytes where need arises, even though the only men so installed are candidates for ordination to the permanent or transitional diaconate.

read as admonitions to deaconesses as well, especially if only a
few widows were ordained as deaconesses in a given local Church.
What might be more telling here regarding the changing understanding of women's ministry is the change in the ministerial
assignments of women.

The ministry of women was controversial even in the early Church.

Women of the Church, no matter how they were described or determined, were increasingly directed to prayer as their service to
the Church. This noteworthy mission and ministry, particularly if
ordered by the bishop, would coincidentally remove women from
active works of charity and involvement in sacramental ministry,
including and especially their ceremonial ministry at baptism.
Polycarp's letter to the Philippians is illustrative of this point:

> And the widows should be discreet in their faith pledged to the
> Lord, praying unceasingly on behalf of all, refraining from all
> slander, gossip, false witness, love of money — in fact, from
> evil of any kind — knowing that they are God's altar, that
> everything is examined for blemishes, and nothing escapes him
> whether of thoughts or sentiments, or any of the secrets of the
> heart.[179]

The conflation of all women's ministries to a single ministry of
prayer is often repeated in Church history and practice. In the
third century, Tertullian railed against those women who taught
and baptized, and in *On the Veiling of Virgins* he declared: "It is
not permitted to a woman to speak in Church. Neither may she
teach, baptize, offer, nor claim for herself any function proper to
a man, least of all the sacerdotal office." Tertullian's quoting Paul
here does not extend to women's gift of prophecy; Tertullian "has
already shown that even they [women] have the right to proph-

---

[179]Polycarp of Smyrna, *Ep. to Philippians* 4, 3 (AV 1, 116, 4–9), *Early Christian Fa-*
thers, trans. C. C. Richardson, New York, 1970, 133, as cited in Gryson, *The Ministry of*
Women, 12.

esying,"[180] a seeming unintended contradiction that reflected the belief and practice of the day. Tertullian included women among the clergy, and they occupied a distinct place in community assemblies.[181] The place of widows in the Church was so distinct, in fact, that sinners prostrated themselves before the widows and the priests.[182] Perhaps Paul was referring only to those women who had not received the imposition of hands.

It is fairly clear at this time that the order of widows was gradually developing into a group of women in service to the bishop, which once may have admitted young virgins in scandal to Tertullian. One can infer that the order of virgins was more enclosed and more dedicated to prayer, while the order of widows was not only dedicated to prayer but also had specific functions within the liturgical assembly that probably evidenced their ministries of service.[183] There is speculation that the order of senior widows that developed was an order equivalent to the presbyterate, that is, there is speculation that senior women (widows) were ordained to a class analogous to the presbyters and were considered ecclesiastical dignitaries or as part of the clergy, although not able to offer the Eucharistic sacrifice.[184]

As the third century progressed, it was more and more common in the West for women to be named, rather than ordained, to the order of widows and to be appointed, rather than ordained, to the order of virgins. Ordination of deaconesses seems to have continued. A specific injunction of the Council of Nicea can be

[180]Gryson, *The Ministry of Women*, 19, quoting Tertullian's *De virginibus velandis* 9, 1 *Corpus christianorum, Series latina* 2:1218, 4:1219, 6. Tertullian cites 1 Corinthians 14:34–35 and 1 Corinthians 11:5.

[181]Gryson, *The Ministry of Women*, 21, citing Kalsbach, "Altkirchliche Einrichtung," 73; Huls, "Dienst der vrouw," 72; Jean Daniélou, *The Ministry of Women in the Early Church*, trans. Glyn Simon (Westminster, Md.: Christian Classics, 1961, 1974), 17, originally published as Jean Daniélou, "Le ministère des femmes dans l'Église ancienne," *La Maison Dieu* 61 (1960): 70–96.

[182]Gryson, *The Ministry of Women*, 21, citing Tertullian's *De pudicitia* 13,7 (*Corpus christianorum, Series latina* 1, 1304, 24–31).

[183]Gryson, *The Ministry of Women*, 22, citing Tertullian's *De virginibus velandis* 9, 2–3 (*Corpus christianorum, Series latina* 2, 1219, 15–29).

[184]Richard P. McBrien, *Catholicism*, study edition (Minneapolis: Winston Press, 1981), 849–50, citing Origen, *Homily on Luke 17*, and Tertullian, *On Monogamy*, 11:1, 4; 12:1.

read to require the rebaptism and reordination of women deacons who come to the Church as former followers of Paul of Samosata, a bishop of Antioch deposed for heresy in 269:

> Those who in the past have been enrolled among the clergy, if they appear to be blameless and irreproachable, are to be rebaptized and ordained by the bishop in the catholic church. . . . Similarly with regard to deaconesses and all in general whose names have been included in the roll, the same form shall be observed.[185]

The text specifically points to deaconesses who have been granted the status of deaconess (probably widows who have assumed the title deaconess), and who must therefore be ordained: "We refer to deaconesses who have been granted this status, for they do not receive [may not have otherwise received] any imposition of hands [hand], so that they are in all respects to be numbered among the laity."[186] Discussion about this passage supports and does not support ordination, but alone it can neither prove nor disprove either position.

As noted earlier, to deny that women were sacramentally ordained as deaconesses is to deny as well the sacramental ordination of their male counterparts. The shift in focus of the deacon from service to the Church to service to the bishop takes place during the fourth century. Coincidentally during this century, especially after the Edict of Milan in 313, the concept of sacramental ordination begins to take root.

Gryson notes that ordination by this time was reserved to those who had specific liturgical functions, whereas both widows and

---

[185]"Si qui vero ex his praeterito tempore in clero fuerunt, si quidem inmaculati et inreprehensibiles apparuerunt, baptizati ordinentur ab episcopo ecclesiae catholicae. . . . Similiter autem et de diaconissis et omnio de his, qui in eadem regula versantur, haec forma servabitur. Meminimus autem de diaconissis quae in eodem habitu esse probantur, quod non habeant aliquam manus impositionem, et eo ideo modis omnibus eas inter laicos deputari." First Council of Nicea, in *Decrees of the Ecumenical Councils*, ed. N. P. Tanner (Washington, D.C.: Georgetown University Press, 1990), 15.

[186]First Council of Nicea, in Tanner, *Decrees of the Ecumenical Councils*, 15.

virgins were enjoined to fast and to pray often for the Church.[187] It is important to note that the Synod of Laodicea in Phrygia (341–81) specifically enjoins against the ordination of senior women, presumably those widows whose status was equivalent or assumed to be equivalent to that of the presbyters in certain liturgical functions.[188]

The ordained female diaconate was discontinued, first in the West and then in the East.

The tradition of ordaining women to the diaconate appears to have been discontinued around the fourth century in the West, although it continued for many centuries in the East and the "blessing" of abbesses remained as a clear successor to the ordination of women deacons.

Latin sources, whose exegesis of texts regarding women deacons roundly discouraged the concept of ordained deaconesses, wholly ignored the fact of women deacons in the East and, in fact, are particularly harsh in general toward women. Ambrosiaster, commenting on 1 Corinthians 14:34–35, may be the first to cast the iconic argument:

> "Women should keep silence in the churches." He is now teaching what he omitted before; he had, indeed, prescribed that women should be veiled in church. Now he explains that unless they are quiet and reserved, there is no purpose in their being veiled. For if the image of God is man, and not woman, and if she be subject to man on account of natural law, how much more in church should she be submissive through respect for him who is the representative of (Christ), who Himself is the head of man.[189]

Yet Eastern exegetes do not seem to doubt the fact of deaconesses in their midst. Gryson notes Clement of Alexandria's reference to

---

[187]Gryson, *The Ministry of Women*, 24, citing *Apostolic Tradition*, 30, trans. G. Dix, *The Apostolic Tradition of Hippolytus* (London: SPCK, 1968), 20:1, 30.

[188]C. J. Hefele, "Synod of Laodicea," in *A History of the Councils of the Church*, trans. H. N. Oxenham (Edinburgh: T. & T. Clark, 1896), 2:305–7.

[189]*Commentary on 1 Corinthians, Corpus Scriptorum ecclesiasticorum* 81–82, 163, 3–164, 7, in Gryson, *The Ministry of Women*, 92.

"women deacons"[190] and John Chrysostom, for whom widows are
an ancient and discontinued institution, does not doubt the deaconesses.[191] Neither does Theodore of Mopsuestia or Theodoret of
Cyrus. Greek sources from the fourth through the sixth centuries
continue to refer to women deacons as women deacons, while
Latin canonical sources of this period referred to deaconesses, who
may have been widows as well as ordained deacons, or simply
widows called "deaconesses."

The Council of Carthage (411–12) makes no mention of deaconesses, although the duties of women are specifically noted as
regards virgins and widows: "Widows or virgins consecrated to
God, who are employed at the baptism of women, must be competent to instruct rude and ignorant women how to answer at
their baptism and how to live afterwards," and women are specifically enjoined from baptizing.[192] At this juncture councils begin
to legislate against deaconesses, and specifically against their ordination, as in Canon 25 of the First Synod of Orange (441):
"Deaconesses are absolutely not to be ordained; and if there are
still any of them, let them bow their heads under the benediction
which is given to the congregation."[193] It is important to note here,
as elsewhere, that there is never any enjoining against the validity
of the ordination of a woman to the diaconate, merely against its
ecclesiastical legality and continuance. Clearly, women had been
ordained, even if the practice was now to stop. In any event, the
canon seems contradicted by the Council of Chalcedon (451),
which states:

> No woman under forty years of age is to be ordained a deacon,
> and then only after close scrutiny. If after receiving ordina-

---

[190]Gryson, *The Ministry of Women*, 30, citing Clement of Alexandria, *Stromata* 3, 6,
53, 3–4, *Griechischen christlichen Schriftsteller*, trans. J. E. L. Oulton and H. Chadwick,
Alexandrian Christianity, Library of Christian Classics 2:65.

[191]Gryson, *The Ministry of Women*, 84–85.

[192]Hefele, "The First Four Carthaginian Synods," in *A History of the Councils*, 412, 417.

[193]Gryson, *The Ministry of Women*, 102, citing First Council of Orange (441), Canon 25
(26) (*Corpus christianorum, Series latina*) 148, 84, 102–3. Another translation: "Deaconesses
shall no longer be ordained, and (in divine service) they shall receive the benediction only
in common with the laity (not among those holding clerical offices)." Hefele, "Synod at
Orange, A.D. 441," in *A History of the Councils*, 163.

tion and spending some time in the ministry she despises God's grace and gets married, such a person is to be anathematized along with her spouse.[194]

Similar injunction against marriage is held in another canon from Chalcedon: "It is not permitted for a virgin who has dedicated herself to the Lord God, or similarly for a monk, to contract marriage."[195] This latter canon more specifically refers to vows, as opposed to orders, as impediments to marriage, but serves to present separate considerations for women deacons and for those in the order of virgins.

The office of deaconess continued to be suppressed, especially at the Synod of Epaon (517) and the Second Synod at Orléans (533) in the West. The force of the status of deaconess is clear in the Orléans canons, for deaconesses who remarry must be excommunicated (this assumes deaconesses who are widows). This Synod also decreed that "to no woman must henceforth the *bene-dictio diaconalis* be given, because of the weakness of the sex,"[196] which could indicate either that no additional women were to be appointed, or that women were no longer to be solemnly ordained. Despite this injunction, women in the West continued to be created deacons, usually as an additional blessing due an abbess. Whether or not understood as ordination that included receipt of sacramental power, the ceremony signified the receipt of juridical power, necessary for the abbess of a territorial monastery. For example, St. Radegund (520–87) was consecrated a deaconess by Medard, Bishop of Noyon, in 555, by the imposition of hands.[197]

---

[194]"Council of Chalcedon–451" in Tanner, *Decrees of the Ecumenical Councils*, 94. This council refers to Canon 19 of the Council of Nicea and Basil of Caesarea, Canon 44. The further question arises: was the Council in the East aware of the Council in the West?

[195]"Council of Chalcedon–451" in Tanner, *Decrees of the Ecumenical Councils*, 94. This council refers to the Council of Ancyra (314), Canon 19, Council of Carthage (419), Canon 16; and Basil of Caesarea, Canons 6, 18–20, 60.

[196]Hefele, "Second Synod at Orléans, AD 533," in *A History of the Councils*, 187.

[197]Paul-Henri LaFontaine, "Le sexe masculin, condition de l'accession aux ordres aux IVe et Ve siècles," *Revue de l'Université d'Ottawa* 31 (1961): 137*–182*, 157*, citing V. Fortunate, *Vita sanctae Radegundis*, cap. 12: "...manu superimposita, consecravit diaconam." See also Hefele, "Synod of Laodicea," A *History of the Councils*, 306–7.

Importantly, the female diaconate is recognized in the East as late as the seventh century Synod in Trullo (the Quinisext Synod, 692),[198] which set the age for the ordination of a deaconess at forty.[199] Those women ordained deaconesses at that time were held in the same restriction against marriage as others who were ordained. That women so ordained to the office of deaconess were considered clergy is clear from the prohibition against marriage; canonical commentaries as late as 1916 include women in an "Excursus on the Marriage of the Clergy" in a commentary on Trullo or Quinisext (692), noting Chalcedon: "A deaconess who marries is to be anathematized (Chal. xv); a monk or dedicated virgin who marries is to be excommunicated (Chal. vi)."[200] The serious distinction between orders and vows, as known by Chalcedon and repeated by Trullo or Quinisext, refutes the concept that the ordination of a deaconess was merely another way of speaking about the consecration of a virgin.

Further, at Trullo or Quinisext, there is a separate admonition against women speaking during divine service (citing 1 Cor. 14:34ff.); this canon comes after canons forbidding lay persons to speak or teach. ("No layman may publicly, in religious services, come forward as speaker or teacher, under penalty of excommunication for forty days.")[201] The implication here at Trullo or Quinisext is that clerics (male) are distinguished from non-clerics (laymen), but that all women come under this prohibition, whether deaconesses or not. The prohibition presents a further barrier to women's ministry, but does not negate the probability that women did receive the imposition of hands that would allow them to speak. The requirement for the imposition of hands for speaking and teaching in the assembly is a constant; women who

---

[198]Hefele, "Synod of Laodicea," in A *History of the Councils*, 306–7.

[199]"In accordance with the ancient laws, no one shall be ordained priest before thirty years, or deacon before twenty-five. A deaconess must be forty years old" (Canon 14). Hefele, "The Quinisext or Trullan Synod, AD 692," A *History of the Councils*, 226.

[200]Philip Schaff and Henry Wallace, eds., A *Select Library of Nicene and Post-Nicene Fathers of the Christian Church, Second Series*, 14 (New York: Charles Scribner's Sons, 1916), 365.

[201]Hefele, "The Quinisext or Trullan Synod, AD 692," in A *History of the Councils*, 232.

by Paul were forbidden to speak in the assembly (cf. 1 Cor. 14:34ff., as above) may have been those who were not so ordained. Canon 14 of the Second Council of Nicaea (787) explicitly notes: "Without the imposition of hands no person should read from the ambo during the church service."[202]

Eventually, only abbesses retained juridical authority due to equal or equivalent clerical status.

As the restrictions relative to teaching and speaking developed and were increasingly tied to ordained status, fewer and fewer women were ordained deaconesses. In fact, as restrictions relative to the three levels of teaching (catechesis, reading the Gospel, and interpreting the scriptures, or preaching) grew, so did the juridical rights of independent monasteries, their abbots and abbesses. That is, each level of teaching depended upon a certain amount of juridical deputation: only those properly authorized could become catechists, those further authorized could proclaim scripture, and those even further authorized could explain scripture, or preach. These distinctions roughly equate to catechist, lector, and priest (or deacon with faculties for preaching), with their concomitant ascending juridical implications.

The beginnings of the understandings of abbots (and abbesses) as juridically equivalent to bishops present themselves just as the rite of ordination for women seems to have disappeared except insofar as it was included in the installation of an abbess, who by right and title had juridical authority. Such juridical authority remained tied to orders, and so her accession to the position of abbess necessarily included at least her "benediction" if not "ordination" as deaconess. The point was to allow her to share in juridical authority and, in fact, to have juridical authority over clerics within her territories.

The distinction between the juridical rights of the head of a monastery, independent of the juridical authority of the bishop

---

[202]"Quod non oporteat sine manus impositione legere in collecta super ambonem." A note refers to the Council of Carthage (419), Canon 16, as well as the Quinisext Council (692), Canon 33. Tanner, *Decrees of the Ecumenical Councils,* 149.

within whose diocese the monastery lay, grew along with the development of the juridical society of the Church. Canons of the Council of Chalcedon (451) solidified subjection of monks to the local bishop, although monastic exemption continued to be claimed and soon became codified. At the Council of Arles (455), the rights and powers of the abbot of Lérin were affirmed over the authority of Bishop Frégus. Nearly concurrently, the Celtic Church affirmed the preeminence of abbots and abbesses over bishops of Iona and Kildare.[203] While the juridical question fell variously to the advantage of abbeys and abbesses, or to bishops, Pope Gregory the Great (590–604) established the exemption of monasteries, men's as well as women's. The abbess was to be elected by the nuns and ordained by the bishop, as in the case of Gregory the Great's letter to Respecta, abbess of the Cassian monastery in Marseilles: "...sed quam congregatio sibi de suis elegerit, ordinatur."[204]

The Bull of Pope Honorius I (625–38) placed the monastery of Bobbio, founded by the Irish monk Columban, outside the jurisdiction of the bishop of Tortona, which exemption was confirmed by Pope Theodore I (642–49) and which essentially carries to this day.[205] The histories of other monasteries in France (Notre-Dame de Jouarre, Faremoutier, and Rebais), Germany (Nivelles, Gandersheim, Cologne, Neuss, Villach, Diedenkirchen), Italy (Conversano, Brindisi), and Spain (Las Huelgas de Burgos) show

---

[203] Joan Morris, *The Lady Was a Bishop: The Hidden History of Women with Clerical Ordination and the Jurisdiction of Bishops* (New York: Macmillan, 1973), 19, citing Venerable Bede, *History of the English Church and People*, trans. Leo Shirley-Price (1956), Book III; Cogitosus, "Vita Sanctae Brigidae," in Thomas Messingham, *Florilegium Insulae Sanctorum seu Vitae et Acta Sanctorum Hiberniae* (Paris: Cramoise, 1624), 193; J. Ryan, *Irish Monasticism* (London: Longman, Green, 1931), 163–90.

[204] "Gregorius Respectae abbatissae de Gallia Maxiliaeu" (Gregorii I. papae registr. VII, 12: Mon. germ. hist. Epp. I p. 454 sq.), in Josephine Mayer, *Monumenta de viduis diaconissis virginibusque tractantia* (Bonn: P. Hanstein, 1938), 49.

[205] R. Kevin Seasoltz, O.S.B., "Institutes of Consecrated Life and Ordained Ministry," in *A Concert of Charisms: Ordained Ministry in Religious Life*, ed. Paul K. Hennessey, C.F.C. (Mahwah, N.J.: Paulist Press, 1997), 142–43. Seasoltz called the exemption of Bobbio "the first exemption of religious in the history of the church" (142), perhaps overlooking the prior exemption in Gregory the Great's letter to Respecta. See also David J. Kay, *Exemption: Origins of Exemption and Vatican Council II* (Rome: Pontifical Gregorian University, 1990).

a quasi-episcopal jurisdiction by abbesses, often confirmed by their winning litigation against local bishops.[206]

Jurisdictions by women waned by the fifteenth and sixteenth centuries and suffered the two-pronged attack on women of the Reformation[207] and of the Council of Trent (1545–63). Even so, royal abbeys (the Cistercian abbeys of Las Huelgas de Burgos and St. Benedict of Conversano, and the Benedictine abbeys Notre-Dame de Jouarre and Fontevrault) and some other Benedictine abbeys (Brindisi, Bari, Oria, and others in Apulia, Italy) maintained their jurisdictional independence up to the early eighteenth century. Las Huelgas lost the right in 1874.[208]

The retention of clear juridical authority (even over clerics) by women up to modern times gives powerful evidence to the Church's understanding that women may be ordained deacons, included in the roster of clerics, and thereby have the ability to hold juridical authority and powers once again, exclusive of their elective office of abbess or prioress.

Summary

The arguments of the prior chapter, from tradition and theology, are supported by scripture and history. However, even in light of scripture, tradition, and theology, the interpretation of historical evidence has been challenged. Yet, the female diaconate as present in scripture and tradition reinforces the historical evidence of women deacons. The early Church evidenced women deacons, although some argue that distinct ministries separate men and women in the order of deacons. In fact, the ministry of women was controversial even in the early Church, and the ordained female diaconate was discontinued, first in the West and then in the East. Eventually, only abbesses retained juridical authority due to

---

[206]Morris, *The Lady Was a Bishop*, chapters 6, 7, 8, 9.

[207]John Knox, *The First Blast of the Trumpet against the Monstrous Regiment of Women*, 1557, would be one example.

[208]"In the cases of the Abbey of Las Huelgas and St. Benedict of Conversano, both maintained exemption not only due to their being royal abbeys but also because they each belonged to a General Chapter of the Cistercian Congregation." Morris, *The Lady Was a Bishop*, 155–57, 156.

equal or equivalent clerical status. Hence, there are stronger arguments from scripture, history, tradition, and theology that women may be ordained deacons than that women may not be ordained deacons.

VI. Women have continually served the Church in diaconal ministry, whether ordained to such service or not.

The historical fact of women deacons in the early Church is incontrovertible.

Retention of juridical authority by abbesses, examined in the prior chapter, is an incontrovertible remnant of the ordination of women to the diaconate and their concomitant clerical status. However, the early Church had not yet developed the categories now extant, so it is necessary to examine the history of women's diaconal ministry, whether ordained to such service or not.

The women who followed Jesus as successors to Mary Magdalene, Joanna, the wife of Chuza, Susanna, and many others (Luke 8:2–3), heeded the repeated call to service. They too were the sons of God, as they heard their dignity proclaimed and recognized their own lives could be sanctified. The old law would no longer apply, and with Jesus' teachings women gained a new dignity. Women were setting out on the difficult road that still lies ahead.

As Jean Daniélou found:

> Some degree of antifeminism, very obvious in Tertullian for example, which one finds in the Middle Ages, and which derives from a somewhat contemptuous attitude towards women or for their lower status (sociologically speaking), certainly had the effect, at certain periods, of putting restrictions upon even the legitimate female ministries.[209]

Daniélou finds four categories for the ministry of women, organized by the early Church into the work of the deaconess: (1) all matters pertaining to religious instruction, excepting official teaching to the Church (including preaching to unchurched

---

[209]Daniélou, *The Ministry of Women*, 28: "Un certain antiféminisme, patent chez un Tertullien, que l'on retrouve au moyen âge, et qui procède d'un certain mépris de la femme ou de sa place subordonnée sociologiquement, a certainement joué à certaines époques pour restreindre les ministères féminins même légitimes." "Le ministère des femmes," 92–93.

women), missionary work, preparation for baptism and the cat-
echumenate (including the giving of spiritual direction), giving
religious instruction to adolescents, children, and within religious
communities; (2) certain functions relative to worship (including
assisting the bishop during the baptism of women — not limited to
anointing and clothing), acting as doorkeeper to the congregation,
oversight of the women's group of the congregation and regulation
of movement in the assembly (especially in connection with the
kiss of peace), preparation of the chalice and self-communication
with it and, in the absence of the priest and deacon, the right
to ascend to the ambo to cense the book, read the Gospel, and
to distribute communion to women and children; (3) all matters pertaining to the care of the sick, including the liturgical
actions of laying on of hands (Daniélou interprets this to include
extreme unction, citing Epiphanius)[210]; and (4) all matters connected with liturgical prayer, especially the chanting of the psalms.
Daniélou finds no duties of the minor orders to have been withheld from women.[211] To be sure, there are those who disagree,
especially Martimort, who argues that the liturgical functions of
deaconesses were strictly limited. Even so, Martimort agrees that
women deacons participated in apostolic ministry, visiting the sick
and engaging in catechetical and charitable activities.[212]

---

[210]"We must remember, however, that the care of the sick is clearly also amongst the
duties of the Deacons and has therefore a certain ministerial side to it as well, moreover, this
assistance involves liturgical actions, such as the laying-on-of-hands. It is in this context
that we must examine the sacrament of extreme unction. It is plain that it could not be
administered to the sick woman by a priest or [male] deacon. Ought we not then to think
that in fact it was administered by the Deaconess and that it is this which is meant when
we have allusions to the laying-on-of-hands by them? Epiphanius' formulation of it is full.
He writes: 'Because of feminine modesty, it may be at the time of Baptism, it may be in
connection with the care of the sick, it may be on every occasion on which the female
body has to be uncovered, the Deaconess is delegated by the priest to perform his ministry
for him, so that the decorum and discretion which are appropriate to the Church may be
safeguarded in such degree as her Law allows'" (79,3). Daniélou, *The Ministry of Women*,
29; "Le ministère des femmes," 94.

[211]Daniélou, *The Ministry of Women*, 29–30: "Je dirai donc que je ne vois aucune des
fonctions qui sont celles des ordres mineurs qui ne puise être assumée par des femmes,
en ce qui concerne leur aspect féminin, et qui en fait ne l'ait été." "Le ministère des
femmes," 94.

[212]"Instituées par un rite liturgique d'après les *Constitutions Apostoliques*, les diaconesses
ont des fonctions liturgiques, mais strictement limitées: elles n'ont aucun rôle dans

Women's diaconal ministry continued throughout the Middle Ages.

The historical evidence of women's diaconal ministry in the Church, as shown in the prior chapter, evidenced a singular dignity to and respect for the ministry of women. This respect waned during the early Middle Ages. By the Middle Ages, women who wished to formally devote their lives to God and God's people were generally restricted to monasteries. Those who served outside those structures lived and died as the poor they served, for the most part without legacies. The great works credited to women in the eleventh and twelfth centuries by and large are known because of their monastic affiliations. Hildegard of Bingen (1098–1179), whose writings included homilies and medicinal remedies, drew large numbers of visitors from France and from Germany who came to her for advice and counsel. At Helfta in Germany, the mystic Mechtilde of Magdeburg (1210–97) and Gertrude the Great (1256–1302) lived their lives in monasteries.

However, against the backdrop of enclosure, silhouetted by the great monasteries of Europe, women continued to find apostolic or active vocations and work in diaconal roles. The Beguines, for example, were active in Belgium and, later, parts of France, from the end of the twelfth century until the fifteenth century. During the fourteenth century, Catherine of Siena gave example to unenclosed life of prayer and service, while in England around the same time two strikingly different women, Julian of Norwich and Margery Kempe, each worked alone in forms of active ministry. By the sixteenth century, what would otherwise be seen as women's diaconal ministry came to be expressed in religious institutes dedicated to active ministry. Two founders of the early seventeenth

l'assemblée, sinon parfois une charge d'accueil et de surveillance des femmes; elles font les onctions de huile d'exorcisme au baptême des femmes, mais ce ne sont pas elles qui baptisent. Elles vont à domicile visiter les malades, elles ont une certaine activité catéchétique et surtout caritative. Sauf dans des sectes hérétiques, jamais il n'a été envisage de promouvoir des femmes au presbytèrat ou à l'épiscopat." Aimé Georges Martimort, "A propos des ministères féminins dans L'Église," *Bulletin de littérature ecclésiastique* 74 (1972–73): 103–8, 104.

century, Mary Ward and Janes Frances de Chantal, both sought
to meet the need for active ministry by unenclosed women.

Until the sixteenth century, each of these included two elements of contemporary diaconal ministry: secular status (for the
most part) and active works. By the 1550s, however, Church
authority sought to organize and legitimize active ministry by
women not with diaconal orders, but through simple (as opposed
to solemn) vows.

The Beguines. The official requirement of enclosure did not
suppress the desire of women to serve as contemporary apostles
to their worlds. One way this desire for service was lived was
through the establishment of noncanonical communities, or at
least groupings, of secular women. Perhaps the best known of
these throughout the late Middle Ages, the Beguinages, were
first established in the Diocese of Liège in Belgium at the end
of the twelfth century. They seem to mark a transmutation of the
historical diaconate of women.

A Belgian priest, Lambert le Begue, built several small houses
around his Church and gave them to women who lived in evangelical simplicity alone or in various communal arrangements as
seculars, and cared for the sick.[213] The Beguines, as they came to
be known, grew in number and adopted a "middle way" without a
specific religious rule, living lives of prayer and service either alone
or conventually, involved both in works of charity and in contemplation. They lived simply in cities, without excluding ownership
of private property, but did establish enclaves that were like secular monasteries. Their living arrangements varied according to
circumstance: some lived communally, some in twos or threes,
some alone. Their work and their conventual and solitary prayer
also varied. They were respected, at least for a time.

Many Beguines lived an apostolic life. A charismatic preacher
of the time, Jacques de Vitry, recorded the life of Marie d'Oignies,

---

[213]Elizabeth Meredith Lee, *As among the Methodists: Deaconesses Yesterday, Today, and Tomorrow* (New York: Board of Missions, The Methodist Church, 1963), 12.

making her the best-known member of the movement. Some of what he recorded reflects earlier understandings of diaconal ministry:

> Therefore, from the abundant piety of her heart she busied her-self as far as she was able in the external works of mercy. But in these works of mercy, she above all occupied herself in assisting the sick and being present at death beds for contrition.[214]

The Beguines were known as well for their learning and their piety. Beatrice of Nazareth (1200–1268) was sent by her father to the Beguines at Leau (Zoutleeuw) at the age of eight or nine. She later went to the Cistercian convent at Florival, where she was professed in 1216. Her writing on the "Seven Steps of Love" explicitly presents the necessity for deeds to act out the love of God:

> Then the beauty of love has bedecked her, the power of love has devoured her, the sweetness of love has submerged her, the grandeur of love has consumed her, the nobility of love has enveloped her, the purity of love has adorned her, and the sublimity of love has drawn her upwards and so united herself with her that she always must be love and do nothing but the deeds of love.[215]

The "deeds of love" would expand beyond prayer to every act of service.

The Beguines enjoyed good repute in their early years; in 1217 St. Francis of Assisi led a pilgrimage to the Diocese of Liège to visit them.[216] They flourished even as the Fourth Lateran Council (1251) forbade the founding of new religious orders, decreeing that only those rules already approved could be used to found

---

[214]Jacques de Vitry, *The Life of Marie d'Oignies*, trans. Margot H. King (Saskatoon, Saskatchewan: Peregrina Publishing, 1986), 51.

[215]Beatrice of Nazareth, "The Power of Love," in *Beguine Spirituality: Mystical Writings of Mechtild of Magdeburg, Beatrice of Nazareth and Hadewijch of Brabant*, ed. Fiona Bowie, trans. Oliver Davies (New York: Crossroad, 1990); Phyllis Zagano, *Woman to Woman: An Anthology of Women's Spiritualities* (Collegeville, Minn.: Liturgical Press, 1993), 10.

[216]de Vitry, *The Life of Marie d'Oignies*, ii.

new houses. (Included implicitly in this decree were the rules of Augustine, Basil, Benedict, and probably Francis.)

The Beguines also grew to threaten the power of Church authority, and they were officially accused of theological speculation and of reading religious writings for which they were not prepared. One of their number, Marguerite de Porete, was known for her mystical writings and her denunciations of the weaknesses of the Church. Her "Mirror for Simple Souls" continued to circulate among monasteries and convents in its original French, and in Latin and English despite the fact that her work had been condemned by the Bishop of Cambrai in Belgium at the turn of the thirteenth century. His successor had de Porete arrested around 1307. Taken to Paris, she refused to answer her accusers. Her work is not unlike other female mystics; her position as a Beguine — unenclosed and essentially untouchable by male Church authority — made her more threatening and therefore more suspect. She was burnt in Paris in 1310.[217] Soon after, the Council of Vienne (1311–12) definitively ruled against the Beguine way of life:

> The women commonly known as Beguines, since they promise obedience to nobody, nor renounce possessions, nor profess any approved rule, are not religious at all, although they wear the special dress of Beguines and attach themselves to certain religious to whom they have a special attraction. We have heard from trustworthy sources that there are some Beguines who seem to be led by a particular insanity. They argue and preach on the holy trinity and the divine essence, and express opinions contrary to the catholic faith with regard to the articles of faith and the sacraments of the church. These Beguines thus ensnare many simple people, leading them into various errors. They generate numerous other dangers to souls under the cloak of sanctity. We have frequently received unfavorable reports of their teaching and justly regard them with suspicion. With the approval of the sacred council, we perpetually forbid their mode of life and remove it completely from the church of God. We expressly enjoin on these and other women, under pain

---

[217]*Beguine Spirituality*, ed. Bowie, 38–39.

of excommunication to be incurred automatically, that they no longer follow this way of life under any form, even if they adopted it long ago, or take it up anew. We strictly forbid, under the same penalty, the religious mentioned above, who are said to have favored these women and persuaded them to adopt the Beguinage way of life, to give in any way counsel, help or favor to women already following this way of life or taking it up anew; no privilege is to avail against the above. Of course we in no way intend by the foregoing to forbid any faithful women, whether they promise chastity or not, from living uprightly in their hospices, wishing to live a life of penance and serving the Lord of hosts in a spirit of humility. This they may do, as the Lord inspires them.[218]

In 1317 Pope John XXII further declared that *status beginarum* could not have official approval. His action was in concert with the widespread repression of religious orders at this time, obviously an attempt to regain juridical control, in the midst of the quarrels among and between bishops, the Franciscans, Rome, and Louis of Bavaria. In order to obtain or retain some status, many individual communities of Beguines later adopted one or another older monastic rule, without giving up the combined devotion to contemplation and works of charity during the structurally disconcerting fourteenth and fifteenth centuries. The Beguine movement as it was known died out in the fifteenth century.[219]

Catherine of Siena. Apostolic work by women in these centuries did not end with the dying out of the Beguines; it then was organized differently, according to the Third Orders developed for women. For example, in Italy, Catherine of Siena (1347–80), who vowed herself to Christ long before she took up the works of a Mantellata, or Third Order Dominican, performed works of

---

[218]Tanner, *Decrees of the Ecumenical Councils,* 374.

[219]The question might arise whether the Beguines would have been helped or hindered by diaconal orders, and the answer is, probably both. No matter which, they present another way of women's organizing ministry and serve as precursors in part to what should become a modern female diaconate.

mercy for the sick and the poor. She had long wanted to disguise herself as a man and take up the Dominican habit, but took
up the clothing of a Dominican Tertiary instead. Her Dominican
confessor, Raymond of Capua, records her conversation with the
Lord on this matter:

> Remember how you used to plan to take up man's attire and
> enter the Order of Preachers in foreign parts to labor for the
> good of souls? Why then are you surprised, why are you sad,
> because I am now drawing you to the work which you have
> longed for from your infancy?[220]

To be sure, Catherine protests, but the Lord responds: "No thing
is impossible with God.... With me there is no longer male and
female ... for all stand equal in my sight, and all things are equally
in my power to do."[221] Catherine's words and works, marked by
her freedom of movement, clearly exemplify a type of diaconal
ministry by a woman for her time.

Julian of Norwich and Margery Kempe. In England, Julian
of Norwich (1342–1423) took up her anchorhold at the age of
thirty, and remained there.[222] Her ministry was one of advice
and counsel, and one who came to her for spiritual counsel was
Margery Kempe of Lynne (c. 1373–c. 1440), the illiterate mother
of fourteen whose way of life comprised contemplation, active
works, pilgrimage, and a somewhat excessive piety.[223] Julian's life,
while enclosed, included active ministry — the giving of spiritual
direction to women (and probably men, too). Her more active

---

[220]Raymond of Capua, *The Life of Catherine of Sienna,* trans. Conleth Kearns, O.P.
(Wilmington, Del.: Michael Glazier, 1980), part 2, chapter 1, nos. 121–22; 116.

[221]Raymond of Capua, *The Life of Catherine of Sienna,* 116.

[222]"The most important independent witness to Julian's historicity is the egregious
Margery Kempe.... The teaching and the techniques recorded by Margery in her account
agree with what we find in Julian's writings." Julian of Norwich, *Showings,* trans. Edmund
Colledge, O.S.A., and James Walsh, S.J. (New York: Paulist Press, 1978), 18.

[223]"The anchoress and I had a great deal of holy conversation as we talked about
the love of our Lord Jesus Christ during the many days we were together." *The Book of
Margery Kempe: The Autobiography of the Madwoman of God,* trans. Tony D. Triggs (Liguori,
Mo.: Triumph Books, 1995), 49. Kempe dictated her autobiography — the first known in
English — between 1434 and 1436.

contemporary, Margery, known for her prayerful excesses, all the
while concerned herself with apostolic works and "preaching," as
she might. When questioned about her life by the Archbishop of
York, Margery answered, "I don't preach, sir; I enter no pulpits.
All I do is talk to people and tell them things that are good for
their souls, and I'll do the same for as long as I live."[224]

Margery lived in the interesting extracanonical world of
fifteenth-century laity and took upon herself the obligation to
speak openly of God, here without benefit of (or thought to)
orders.

Women's diaconal ministry came to be expressed in organized apostolic institutes.

Whether wandering alone in pilgrimage, or living alone in anchor-
holds, or together in Third Orders, women continued to serve
the ministerial needs of the Church. For the most part, there was
little Church approval for direct affiliation of women to meet a
specific need through active ministry until the sixteenth century,
although their work continued throughout. One could argue that
Gregory XIII's acknowledgement of simple vows in 1550 allowed
women to group themselves into communities specifically for the
purpose of active service in the world, the beginnings of "active"
or "apostolic" congregations (as opposed to secular Third Orders).
Such a manner of religious life was not necessarily restricted to a
contemplative and monastic existence with the solemn vows of an
order and the strict *clausura* of the Council of Trent (1563), which
was solidified by Pius V's *Circa Pastoralis* (1566), but it was the
opening of an additional avenue within the Church for women's
continued apostolic ministry, albeit unordained by this time.

At this juncture, however, it is well to recall that canonical
monasteries of contemplative women continued their missions of
prayer for the Church, and their prayer comprised the liturgy of
the hours, which was increasingly becoming an obligation of the
clergy. That is, some of the liturgical duties of the clergy remained

---

[224] *The Book of Margery Kempe*, 113.

with women, while women exercised the ministerial work of clergy (of deacons, if there had been many deacons at the time) as well.

Mary Ward. There was no immediacy in the development of apostolic institutes of women religious however. What came to be known as the Institute of the Blessed Virgin Mary, the "English Ladies" founded by Mary Ward in 1609, survived suppressions and even the imprisonment of its founder. Through a powerful spiritual experience, Mary Ward in 1611 understood she was to "take the same of the Society," that is, to adopt the rule of the Society of Jesus (the Jesuits), which had been founded in 1541 as a clerical society:

> About this time in the year 1611 I fell sick in great extremity; being somewhat recovered (by a vow made to send in pilgrimage to our Blessed Lady of Sichem), being alone, in some extraordinary response of mind, I heard distinctly, not by sound of voice but intellectually understood, these words: Take the same of the Society, so understood as that we were to take the same both in matter and manner, that only excepted which God by diversity of sex hath prohibited. . . . My confessor resisted, all the Society opposed; diverse institutes were drawn by several persons, some of which were approved and greatly commended by the last Bishop Blasius of Saint Omers, our so great friend, and some other divines. These were offered us and as it were pressed upon us; there was no remedy but refuse them, which caused infinite troubles. These would they needs that at least we should take the name of some order confirmed, or some new one, or any we could think of, so not that of Jesus. This the Fathers of the Society urged exceedingly (and do still every day), telling us that to any such name we may take what constitutions we will, even theirs in substance, if otherwise we will not be satisfied; but by no means will they that we observe that form which their constitutions are written in. . . . [this] cause[d] extreme troubles, especially for the first 7 years.[225]

---

[225]Mary Ward, "Letter to the Apostolic Nuncio of Lower Germany, Msgr. Albergato, 1620," from manuscript transcriptions of the Archives of the Institute of the Blessed Virgin Mary, trans. Phyllis Zagano with their approval, in Zagano, *Woman to Woman*, 58–59.

Mary Ward endured multiple hardships and tragedies in her quest to form an apostolic group of women. She did adapt the Jesuit *Formula Instituti* as the rule for her institute, and walked from Brussels to Rome to present it to Pope Gregory XV in 1621; she futilely awaited the rule's approval even as her houses multiplied. In 1631, the Institute was suppressed, its property confiscated, and Mary Ward was jailed as a heretic by the Inquisition. The three hundred women of the Institute clung together, and their apostolic lives and those of their successors waxed and waned for over 250 years. It was not until 1907 that Pius X gave retroactive sanction to this institute (recognizing Mary Ward as its founder) and thereby implicitly sanctioning other expressions of "apostolic" congregations.

As it was, in the seventeenth century women's expression of prayer and service to the People of God, arguably descendent from the historic diaconate (male and female), was stymied by Church authority, which required they use previously approved constitutions and rules, including those belonging to men who were apparently unwilling to share them freely. Just as post-Tridentine theology denied women jurisdiction, so post-Tridentine sociology denied women ministerial presence outside the monastery or convent. As Mary Milligan has pointed out, the papal decree of enclosure in 1566, had solidified

> ...cloister as an integral part of feminine religious life and only those with solemn vows and cloister were considered "true religious."...There arose, therefore, a number of "apostolic associations" or "reunions," pious unions, groups of women without vows or with only one vow, who were dedicated to the service of the poor, the ignorant, the sick. These associations or "reunions" were not held to common law applying to religious and therefore had a greater freedom of movement.[226]

Freedom of movement, of course, would be necessary to the diaconal works taken up by these associations of women, but Church

---

[226]Mary Milligan, R.S.H.M., "Formation for Ministry in the Church Today" (Ottawa: Religious Formation Conference, 1977), 21.

authority was not so willing to give up the notion that women's ministry must be restricted by enclosure or to restrict such ministry to prayer.

Contemporary needs continued to call women beyond the cloister, but not without danger. Those who lived alone outside of cloister were especially endangered. In Spain, in 1575, "inquisitors investigated Beatas who provided shelter for women with marital troubles, rescued young girls from procuresses, and helped repentant women to marry or find employment as servants."[227] Similar problems arose elsewhere.

Jane Frances de Chantal. The rise of apostolic orders seemed to answer at least one of the complaints, that is, women alone or nonjuridically banding together to do good works did not fit into the Tridentine formula of how a woman might dedicate herself to God. Nearly coincidental to Mary Ward's founding of what became the Institute of the Blessed Virgin Mary, in 1610 Jane Frances de Chantal with Francis de Sales founded the Order of the Visitation of Mary (Visitandines), specifically for the active works of the education of girls and care of the sick.

The specter of plague and other contagious diseases met in ministry to the sick transformed the homeless poor and ill, from persons needing help into threats to the physical and spiritual well-being of the ministering unmarried women who lived and worked outside the cloister. The association of unmarried women with ill men brought scandal, as they were accused of sexual misconduct so much that Francis de Sales ordered his Visitandines to work only with ill women, unless it was absolutely necessary to attend to ill men.[228] By 1618 the Archbishop of Lyons, Cardinal de Marquemont, required the Visitandines' enclosure in order for them to receive ecclesiastical approbation.

---

[227] Jo Ann Kay McNamara, *Sisters in Arms: Catholic Nuns through Two Millennia* (Cambridge, Mass.: Harvard University Press, 1996), 475.

[228] Ibid., 474, citing Francis de Sales, *Oeuvres*, 25:232.

Women's apostolic ministry became further separated from women's juridical authority.

As the essentially diaconal work of women expanded with the development of active religious communities of women, so the juridical privileges of the deaconess outlined earlier, in the East and throughout the West in the Middle Ages, remained within the monastic enclosure and contracted. While the juridical authority of abbesses had been asserted as early as the fifth century and reasserted throughout the early Middle Ages, various portions of their juridic authority were gradually removed. For example, in 1210 Pope Innocent III prohibited Cistercian abbesses in Burgos and Palencia from continuing to bless, hear the confessions of, or preach the Gospel to their religious, the right to which practices flowed from "their having received the blessing and imposition of hands."[229] Even so the abbess of Las Huelgas de Burgos had full and double territorial jurisdiction (temporal and religious), and more or less retained her powers well into the eighteenth century.[230]

While the quasi-episcopal authority of abbesses eroded, most definitively up to the end of the nineteenth century, abbesses and prioresses of enclosed abbeys and monasteries of nuns today retain some juridical authority apparently dually related to their territories and their communities: no bishop, priest, or deacon, may preach there without the permission of the abbess or prioress.[231] The recent document of the Congregation for Institutes of Consecrated Life and Societies of Apostolic Life, "*Verbi Sponsa:* Instruction on the Contemplative Life and on the Enclosure of

---

[229]"Le Monasticum Cisterciense rappelle la sévère prohibition d'Innocent III, en 1210, contre les abbesses de Burgos et de Palencia, 'qui bénissent leurs religieuses, entendent la confession de leurs péchés, et se permettent de prêcher en lisant l'Évangile.'" Thomassin, *Vetus et nova Eccl. discipl.*, p. 1. III, c. XLVIII, n. 4, in Pie De Langogne, "Abbesses," *Dictionnaire de Théologie Catholique,* ed. A. Vacant and E. Mangenot (Paris: Letouzey et Ané, 1903), 20.

[230]Pie De Langogne, "Abbesses," 22.

[231]Canon 765: "Preaching to religious in their churches or oratories requires the permission of the superior who is competent in accord with the norm of the constitutions." See also Paul VI, Motu proprio *Cum ad motae,* June 11, 1964: *Canon Law Digest* 6 (1963–64): 150.

Nuns," gives abbesses and prioresses authority to temporarily re-
lease enclosed nuns from cloister without permission of the local
bishop or the order's male superior, noting that "in the new vision
and perspective in which the Church today envisages the role
and presence of women, it is necessary to overcome, wherever
it may still exist, that form of juridical supervision by Orders of
men and regular Superiors which *de facto* limits the autonomy of
monasteries of nuns."[232]

Secular canonesses may present a predictive type for the female diaconate.

Juridical authority of women remains solely connected to the office of abbess or prioress, but it appears to have existed as well in
the canoness institutes. Even so, from the remnants of the female
diaconate in the eighth century, in some territories women retained juridical authority connected to the ordination of seculars
as secular canonesses. Members of these institutes sometimes lived
in common, and sometimes privately around an abbey church,
and retained rights to their property. While unrelated to the Beguines, they were not unlike them and Rome similarly refused to
recognize them, and even forbade them. At least two councils,
Chalons (813) and Aachen (816), promulgated rules for "*sancti-
moniales qui se canonicas vocant* (women living a devout life, who
call themselves canonesses)".[233] In some cases, abbeys of secular canonesses pretended to be Benedictine in order to elude
censure by Church authority. Secular canonesses flourished in
Germany, France, and the Netherlands; the abbess of the institute was consecrated by the bishop with a rite similar to that for
a deaconess.[234]

The famous Quedlinburg Institute controlled the entire village,
and its abbess controlled the Quedlinburg Institute. Quedlin-

---

[232]Congregation for Institutes of Consecrated Life and for Societies of Apostolic Life,
"*Verbi Sponsa:* Instruction on the Contemplative Life and on the Enclosure of Nuns,"
(Vatican City: Libreria Editrice Vaticana, 1999), III:26, 34.

[233]N. Backmund, "Canonesses," *New Catholic Encyclopedia* (Washington, D.C.: Catholic University of America, 1967), 53–54, 53.

[234]Ibid.

burg abbesses repeatedly had their right of exemption reaffirmed by several Popes, including John XIII (968), Sylvester II (999), and Lucius III (1184). The aggregate membership was called a canonical institute by Sylvester II (999); individual members were called canonesses, not nuns, by Innocent III (1206). Quedlinburg retained the character of a canoness institute until the Reformation.[235] When Gregory VII sought to regularize all canonical institutes and required they adopt the Rule of St. Augustine, the secular character of many canoness institutes waned.[236]

The canoness institute seems to have marked its membership as clergy, and the ordinary way of entering the clergy has historically been through at least promising ordination. In the case of Quedlinburg, from its founding to its changeover to Protestantism, its abbesses were exempt and its canonesses were ordained and held positions similar to those of the canons.[237]

Other communities of canonesses with apparent juridical authority existed in Europe, roughly between the tenth and fourteenth centuries, for example, at St. Ursula's, Cologne,[238] at Waldreu, Belgium, and at St. Mary's, Überwasser. In some cases, canonesses were recognized as late as the seventeenth and eighteenth centuries, for example, at Remiremont[239] and at

---

[235]Joan Morris, *The Lady Was a Bishop: The Hidden History of Women with Clerical Ordination and the Jurisdiction of Bishops* (New York: Macmillan, 1973), 58–61, citing F. E. Kettner, *Antiquitates Quedlinburgenses* (1712), 222, and J. Fritch, *Geschichte des vormaligen Reichstifts und der Stadt Quedlinburg* (Quedlinburg: Verlag von G. Wasse, 1828), vol. 2.

[236]Backmund, "Canonesses," *New Catholic Encyclopedia,* 53.

[237]Morris, *The Lady Was a Bishop,* 62, 130. Morris's study focuses on the juridical authority of abbesses, and so she does not repeat the ordination ceremonies of canonesses. She quotes a portion of the ceremony in the Mozarabic *Liber Ordinum,* chapter 23, "Ordo ad Ordinandum Abbatissam," which notes that the abbess is to be vested, crowned with a miter, and given the pallium in a ceremony beginning with the words: "Omnipotens Domine Deus, apud quem non est discretio sexuum, nec ulla sanctarum disparilitas animarum…." ("Omnipotent Lord God, before whom there is no difference of sexes, nor any inequality of holy souls….").

[238]Helmut Milner, *Die Bistümer der Kirchenprovinz Köln: Das Bistum Münster,* vol. 5: *Das Kanonissenstift und Benediktinerkloster Liesborn* (Berlin: de Gruyter, 1987). This study encompasses the ninth to the eighteenth centuries.

[239]Marie-Odile Boulard, "Les chanoinesses de Remiremont, du XIVème siècle au début du XVIIème siècle," in *Remiremont, Nancy* (Publications de l'Université de Nancy II, 1980), 61–69.

Notre Dame de Saverne.[240] St. Mary's, Überwasser was a secular canoness community until 1460, an example of the secular
canoness communities that existed to the fifteenth century. From
the sixteenth to eighteenth centuries abbeys of canonesses existed
in Germany and Austria, and, to a certain degree, some still exist.
Other German abbeys of secular canonesses continue to flourish
as *Evangelische Fräuleinstifte*.[241]

The secular canonesses of Germany shared common life as
seculars, much it would seem as celibate secular clerics of today. They were not uniformly vowed or promised to celibacy and
their commitment was not necessarily seen as permanent or separated from the world. If secular canonesses did depart from the
canoness institute, they no longer received the diocesan prebend
(either as money or as board). Their service to the Church consisted in celebration of the office, catechetical work, and running
hospitals.[242]

Canoness institutes have survived in Protestant denomina-
tions, primarily in Germany, and this thread from the past
seems woven into the concurrent growth of Catholic institutes
of apostolic women religious, each dedicated to specific service and charism (e.g., mercy, hope, charity) or spirituality (e.g.,
Franciscan, Benedictine, Dominican) within a framework of the
evangelical counsels. The abundance of charisms and spiritualities bore fruit with the founding of many institutes, most requiring
profession of three vows: poverty, chastity, and obedience. Some
institutes included or sought to include a fourth vow, addressed
to the particular charism of the institute ("zeal," for example), but
the basic public commitment was through the three.

The commentary published by the Leadership Conference of
Women Religious on the Canon Law Society of America report
mentions the rise of women's religious institutes after the definitive end of the diaconate for women, and notes that "from one

---

[240]Octave Meyer, "Le Chapitre Notre Dame de Saverne au XVIIIème siècle," *Archives
de l'Église d'Alsace*, 43 (1984): 143–58.

[241]Backmund, "Canonesses," *New Catholic Encyclopedia*, 53.

[242]Morris, *The Lady Was a Bishop*, 64, 67–68.

point of view it is certainly legitimate to see these varying developments as continuing the diaconal character of ministerial service
within the Christian community and especially as arising under
the impulse of the Holy Spirit."[243]

Women's ministry in modern times includes diaconal service.

With the absorption of the concept of the secular canoness into
the juridical framework of unordained religious life, and with most
of the juridical authority of women retained in the enclosure,
women who sought to salve the needs of the People of God continued to organize themselves as they could, specifically according
to the needs presented by their times.

The modern history of women religious is well known. As Jean
Daniélou has pointed out, from the Third Orders for women in the
Middle Ages up to the nineteenth century's numerical advance
in the numbers of women's communities devoted to missionary
work, religious education, care of the sick, and auxiliary work in
the parishes, it is the women who "provided the answer to those
needs which throughout remain unchanged."[244] Those needs, for
two thousand years, have been recognized and attended to by
some expression of the compassion of Jesus. Women especially
have lived this compassion, whether joining together to respond
to the suffering of the French Revolution, or to the needs of the
dying poor in India one hundred years later. The works of these
institutes of men and women in the nineteenth and twentieth
centuries are recognized as principally responsible for the development of Catholic education and Catholic health care in the
United States. The concurrently developing men's religious institutes were largely clerical, that is, comprised of priests, or of priests

---

[243]Nadine Foley, O.P., *Commentary on the Study by the Canon Law Society of America,
"The Canonical Implications of Ordaining Women to the Permanent Diaconate"* (Silver Spring,
Md.: Leadership Conference of Women Religious, n.d.), 3–4.

[244]Daniélou, *The Ministry of Women*, 31: "...on peut dire que ce sont les religieuses
qui ont été la réponse de fait à des besoins qui sont toujours les mêmes." Daniélou, "Le
ministère des femmes," 61.

and brothers, although they were similarly devoted to education and social service.

Those men's institutes founded as lay institutes mirrored the women's institutes in diaconal intent. Concurrently, in some areas, traditional monastic life retained its tradition of the divine office and contemplative works, but grew to include the "active" ministries of schools, hospitals, and parishes.[245] A majority of the "active" congregations of women were diocesan, and served within a single diocese; some began as such and then became papal,[246] thereby expanding their territorial reach and influence, analogous in some ways to exempt monasteries. Their expansion and development pressed toward more active service. In the early 1970s, the Union of International Superiors General, the membership organization for the leadership of papal congregations, sent a questionnaire to women's congregations worldwide; thirty respondents included their predictions for the future:

> ...most of them tending in the direction of greater participation in the life of the Church and greater solidarity with the poor and the marginalized. First of all, collaboration with the Hierarchy was foreseen as well as certain "ecclesial ministries": the building of christian communities, parish leadership, seminary teaching, the diaconate, the priesthood (mentioned by two countries). Involvement in specifically spiritual ministries was seen as continuing and increasing. As for apostolic insertion, the following milieus were singled out in a special way: youth, the poor, and the working class; also, "those milieus

---

[245]Some monastic foundations erected in mission territories, such as the United States in the nineteenth century, also founded or staffed diocesan parishes, for example, St. Vincent Archabbey, Latrobe, Pa.; St. John's Abbey, Collegeville, Minn.; St. Benedict's Abbey, Atchison, Kans.; and Newark Abbey (formerly St. Mary's Abbey, Newark, N.J.), all of the American Cassinese Congregation.

[246]Papal congregations, especially of women religious, are an interesting case. All began within a single diocese, by leave of the diocesan bishop. Their works expanded to other dioceses, not necessarily as missionaries, but as workers within a given diocese, and they established their own independent organizations — schools, hospitals, social service agencies. Their existence as papal congregations makes them in theory not unlike the personal prelature of Opus Dei, in that they are not territorially bound or governed, and their superiors general hold ultimate juridical power over their members (except insofar as Curial departments will intercede). Men's clerical orders are perhaps even more analogous to the concept of the personal prelature, which essentially organizes and governs seculars.

where the Church is not present." Those who will have a special claim on sisters are: the physically and mentally handicapped, drug addicts, alcoholics, the unemployed, the ignorant, the aged; law offenders, unwed mothers, those suffering with boredom and frustrations of a materialistic society. The importance of addressing the causes of injustice was underlined by some respondents. Finally, some saw increased ecumenical collaboration and collaboration with governments as realities for the future.[247]

Here the twofold nature of the relationship with the Church through consecration, communion, and mission as seen in *Vita Consecrata* is distinguished between "ecclesial ministries," which are directly in relation to the diocesan structure, and "apostolic insertion," which may be also a part of the diocesan structure but is not necessarily such. In either case, the expansion of ministry foreseen by the Union of International Superiors General has slowed somewhat, due to lack of numbers, especially in the developed nations. It is a difficult fact, but perhaps a sign of growth and of health, that in the developed nations institutes of women religious may be dying out, possibly to be reborn as institutes more clearly "religious" (and in one sense extra-diocesan),[248] while the direct service to and within the diocesan structure is taken up by lay persons and married clergy (mostly deacons) and, eventually, by women deacons.

There are fewer than half the number of women religious in the United States today as there were at the time of Vatican II,[249] but, despite shrinking numbers and fewer candidates, religious institutes of women seem determined to survive, specifically as lay

---

[247]Mary Milligan, R.S.H.M., "The Woman Religious and the World: In Search of a Preposition," *USIG Bulletin,* special issue (1975): 80–92, 90.

[248]That is, since apostolic groups of women religious can no longer depend for their work on diocesan structures, they will of needs find other ways of insertion into the realities of Church and world while still living out their specific charisms.

[249]"Between 1965 and 1995, the number of women in religious orders shrank from 179,954 to 92,107, according to the Center for Applied Research in the Apostolate at Georgetown University." Gayle White, "Nuns Have More Ways to Serve but Find Numbers Shrinking," *Atlanta Journal and Constitution,* February 2, 1997, D-10.

religious institutes.[250] Women religious, lay ministers all, do serve in one sense as successors to the ordained women deacons of the early Church, as well as successors to the Third Order women who served so nobly, to secular pilgrims, and to the monastics for whom prayer and asceticism were primary goals and means of service. The lives of some apostolic women religious today can be an expression of diaconal service, but by no means are their lives solely an expression of diaconal service as it is currently understood. Neither ought the individual charisms of religious institutes be overlooked, specifically in their extra-diocesan expressions.

While there remains no method by which women in any category — apostolic religious, seculars, members of Third Orders, contemplatives or monastics — can participate in ordained service to the Church, many of their means of service to the Church, to the People of God and to the Hierarchy, are descendent from roles to which women were previously ordained.

The report of the Canon Law Society of America finds that women can be ordained to the diaconate.

In 1992 the Board of Governors of the Canon Law Society of America established a committee of seven members of the Society[251] to report on the canonical implications of the ordination of women to the permanent diaconate, which resulted in the findings that:

> Women have been ordained permanent deacons in the past, and it would be possible for the Church to determine to do so

---

[250]See, for example, Patricia Wittberg, S.C., *Creating a Future for Religious Life: A Sociological Perspective* (New York: Paulist Press, 1991); David J. Nygren and Miriam D. Ukeritis, *The Future of Religious Orders in the United States: Transformation and Commitment* (Westport, Conn.: Praeger, 1993); Patricia Wittberg, S.C., *Pathways to Re-Creating Religious Communities* (New York: Paulist Press, 1996); and especially Doris Gottemoeller, R.S.M., "The Priesthood: Implications in Consecrated Life for Women," in *A Concert of Charisms: Ordained Ministry in Religious Life,* ed. Paul K. Hennessey, C.F.C. (Mahwah, N.J.: Paulist Press, 1997), 127–38.

[251]Nancy Reynolds and Harmon Skillen, co-chairs, Lucy Blyskal, James A. Coriden, Lynn Jarrell, James H. Provost, and Joseph W. Pokusa, *The Canonical Implications of Ordaining Women to the Permanent Diaconate* (Washington, D.C.: Canon Law Society of America, 1995).

again. Cultural factors were a major element in the decision, in
various local areas of the Church in the past, to ordain women
as permanent deacons; cultural factors continue to be a major
consideration in the decision to ordain men as permanent deacons today, and would be a major element in any decision to
ordain women as permanent deacons in a local area of the
Church.... [Ordination to the diaconate] would provide the
grace of the sacrament for women who are already doing important service in the Church, would open the way for women
to exercise diaconal service in the teaching, sanctifying, and
governing functions of the Church, and would make them capable of holding ecclesiastical office now open to deacons but
closed to lay persons.[252]

To a large extent, the documents used to support the historical
conclusions of the Canon Law Society of America document are
those used by Paul VI in *Ad Pascendum* (1972), which presented
norms for the permanent diaconate,[253] and those used earlier
by Vatican II in discussing the diaconate, particularly *Didascalia
Apostolorum*. The historical summary in the Canon Law Society
document traces numerous examples of women's diaconal ordination and ministry, and finds that the majority of scholars conclude
that women were in fact ordained. The return to the practice
of ordaining women to the permanent diaconate, according to
the writers, "would impart sacramental grace to strengthen the
ministry they already provide in the Church...."[254] Further, the
document concludes, "the ordination of women to the permanent
diaconate is possible, and may even be desirable for the United
States in the present cultural circumstances."[255]

This document joins calls for the inclusion of women in the permanent diaconate as a means of better incorporating the present
service of women in the Church, and marks an important juncture in the development of the understanding that the ordained

---

[252]*The Canonical Implications of Ordaining Women to the Permanent Diaconate*, 1–2.
[253]Paul VI, Apostolic letter *Ad Pascendum* (August 15, 1972).
[254]*The Canonical Implications of Ordaining Women to the Permanent Diaconate*, 35.
[255]Ibid., 51.

ministry of service by women is necessary to the Church, that is, to both the People of God and the Hierarchy.

Summary

The historical fact of women deacons in the early Church is incontrovertible and, while the female diaconate was abandoned as such, women's diaconal ministry continued throughout the Middle Ages. Medieval examples of the ways in which women lived lives of ministry include the Beguines, Catherine of Siena, Julian of Norwich, and Margery Kempe. Women's diaconal ministry eventually came to be expressed in organized apostolic institutes, for example, those founded by Mary Ward and Jane Frances de Chantal. Concurrently, women's apostolic ministry became further separated from women's juridical authority. One joining of the two, in the institutes of secular canonesses, may present a predictive type for the female diaconate. Women's ministry in modern times includes diaconal service. The report of the Canon Law Society of America finds that women can be ordained to the diaconate. Without question, women have continually served the Church in diaconal ministry, whether ordained to such service or not.

VII. The ordained ministry of service by women is necessary to the Church, that is, to both the People of God and the Hierarchy.

Belief in the charism of orders supports the need to include women among the ordained.

The restored permanent diaconate of men has invigorated many of the Church's ministries. As an ordained ministry, it is intimately connected with Christ's mission:

> It [the permanent diaconate] is thus the sacrament of apostolic ministry. The sacramental act of ordination surpasses mere election, designation or delegation by the community, because it confers a gift of the Holy Spirit enabling the exercise of sacred power which can only come from Christ himself through his Church.... The sacramental nature of ecclesial ministry is such that it has "intrinsically linked... its *character of service.* Entirely dependent on Christ who gives mission and authority, ministers are truly 'slaves of Christ' (cf. Rom. 1:11), in the image of him who freely took 'the form of a slave' for us (cf. Phil. 2:7)."[256]

Belief that the sacramental fact of ordination "surpasses mere election, designation or delegation by the community" binds those ordained even more to the whole Church. That is, while the permanent deacon is called forth from a particular local community, he — or she — through incardination would immediately be at the service of the larger community. The exercise of sacred power, therefore, is not in or of the individual or the local community, but in and of "Christ himself through his Church." The "character of service" of the permanent diaconate is truly "dependent on

---

[256]Congregation for Catholic Education and Congregation for the Clergy, "Joint Declaration and Introduction" to *Basic Norms for the Formation of Permanent Deacons and Directory for the Ministry and Life of Permanent Deacons* (Vatican City: Libreria Editrice Vaticana, 1998), para. 1, citing the *Catechism of the Catholic Church,* no. 1536, no. 1538, and no. 876. The inscription of Theoprepeia, a woman deacon of Macedonia, reads: "Here Theoprep(e)ia, the slave of the Lord, eternal virgin and deacon of Christ, who finished an ascetic, zealous, altogether honorable life in God the Lord." Ute E. Eisen, *Women Officeholders in Early Christianity: Epigraphical and Literary Studies,* trans. Linda M. Maloney (Collegeville, Minn.: Liturgical Press, 2000), 178.

Christ" through his Church. Hence, just as it is Christ who raises up the Church, it is Christ who raises up its servants.

The call for the restoration of the permanent diaconate in the Second Vatican Council document *Ad Gentes* stressed the strengthening of the charism of orders, the "laying on of hands," to assist the ministry of those already serving as catechists and in diaconal roles:

> It would help those men who carry out the ministry of dea-
> con — preaching the word of God as catechists, governing
> scattered Christian communities in the name of the bishop or
> parish priest, or exercising charity in the performance of social
> or charitable works — if they were to be strengthened by the im-
> position of hands which has come down from the apostles. They
> would be more closely bound to the altar and their ministry
> would be made more fruitful through the sacramental grace of
> the diaconate.[257]

Additionally, the expressly ecclesial nature of the permanent diaconate presents the fact of ordination as both strengthening and marking acceptance of the ministry of the permanent dea-con. *Sacrum diaconatus ordinem* of Paul VI, which established the canonical norms for the permanent diaconate, underscored the need for the diaconal ministry to be strengthened by sacramental grace.[258]

It would seem that the present diaconal involvements of women could similarly be strengthened by ordination. That is, since the National Conference of Catholic Bishops and individual bishops worldwide find a continued need for a permanent diaconate, it would seem necessary to include women within it. Without question, women's diaconal ministries would be equally enriched and strengthened by the sacramental grace of orders: a new group of devout persons would be enlisted in the apostolic

---

[257] Decree on the Church's Missionary Activity, *Ad Gentes* (December 7, 1995), in *Vatican Council II: The Conciliar and Post Conciliar Documents*, ed. Austin Flannery, O.P. (Wilmington, Del.: Scholarly Resources, 1975), 833.

[258] Paul VI, Motu proprio *Sacrum diaconatus ordinem* (June 18, 1967), *Acta Apostolicae Sedis* 59 (1967): 697–704.

ministry of the Church, liturgical and charitable services would be extended to the faithful, an official and sacramental presence of the Church would be provided both in secular life and in regions where priests are not available, and such would provide both impetus and source for creative adaptations of diaconal ministries to the rapidly changing needs of society.[259] The prior discussions surrounding the restoration of the permanent diaconate, and the inclusion of married men in it, all apply to women.[260]

Ordained diaconal service by women responds to the needs of the whole Church.

An ordained female diaconate would serve the needs of the whole Church, bereft at present of women stably installed to any official ministry of the Church. This recognizes that the diaconate is an inferior grade of the Hierarchy,[261] as well as that the whole Church has the right to the benefits of the grace of the sacrament of orders as it would strengthen the present and future diaconal ministries of women.

These diaconal ministries of women are truly ministries of service. The very permanency of the permanent diaconate mitigates against any thought that it would lead to something else. Permanent deacons, like all ministers, "are truly 'slaves of Christ' (cf.

---

[259]When the National Conference of Catholic Bishops requested the restoration of the permanent diaconate in the United States in 1968, it presented these five areas of need that can equally be applied to women deacons: (1) strengthen current diaconal ministries; (2) enlist new workers to ministry; (3) expand liturgical and charitable services to the People of God; (4) provide official and sacramental presence, especially where priests are not available; (5) provide impetus for creative adaptation of diaconal ministries to the needs of the society. National Conference of Catholic Bishops, Committee on the Permanent Diaconate, *Permanent Deacons in the United States: Guidelines on Their Formation and Ministry*, rev. ed. (Washington, D.C.: United States Catholic Conference, 1984), 1–2. The request, made May 2, 1968, was approved within four months.

[260]See, for example, B. D. Marliangeas, *Clés pour une théologie du ministère: in persona Christi, in persona Ecclesiae* (Paris: Éditions Beauchesne, 1978); P. Winninger and Y. Congar, eds., *Le diacre dans l'Église et le monde d'aujourd'hui* (Paris: Éditions du Cerf, 1966); "A Functional Diaconate: Document Sent to All Bishops by 82 Signatories from 19 Countries," *Worship* 37 (August–September 1963): 513–20; "Le renouveau du diaconat," *Études* 310 (August 1961): 115–19; John Horfinger, "The Case for Permanent Deacons," *Catholic Mind* 57 (April 1959): 114–25.

[261]"At a lower level of the hierarchy are to be found deacons, who receive the imposition of hands...." *Lumen Gentium*, no. 29, in Flannery, *Vatican Council II*, 387.

Rom. 1:11) in the image of him who 'freely took the form of a slave' for us (cf. Phil. 2:7)"[262] and seek to live as such. Beyond, the Christian promise is such that any other foundation to a vocation to the permanent diaconate would be built on sand.

Personal vocation to the ordained permanent diaconate is sup- ported externally and internally by the recognition that the work of the Church is there to be done by all; it is supported and argued (probably unintentionally) by women as different as Mother Teresa and Rosemary Ruether. The crucial point is that the work of the Church must be done by the Church for the Church. Both Mother Teresa and Rosemary Ruether, each representative of a particular view of the way women are in relation to the Church, as deter- mined by culture, faith, experience, and thought, present distinct arguments that are in essence the same. Mother Teresa's belief that the argument about the ordination of women (to priesthood) is unnecessary because there is too much to be done is precisely the same as those who presume that in order to do what ought be done, women would best be ordained to service. Separatist arguments of Rosemary Ruether and others — that women need all-women organizations — do not contribute to critical exegesis of the point, but convey the opposite argument: that the Church as a present structure is unnecessary and redundant. In each schema, women-formed and women-run institutions support the distinct notion that women would best be off forming their own struc- tures to deal with problems inherently female, and consequently creating a governance that speaks only to them.[263] Even so, they argue to create a structure, and all structure eventually requires certification for, and gradations of, membership. The need for all- female structures, however, whether supported by Mother Teresa or by Rosemary Ruether, does not obviate the need for women

---

[262] Congregation for Catholic Education and Congregation for the Clergy, *Basic Norms for the Formation of Permanent Deacons and Directory for the Ministry and Life of Permanent Deacons*, para. 1.

[263] Ruether, *Women-Church*. Another way of viewing this is that women already have created their own self-sufficient structures for ministry, predominantly schools and hospitals, in which they act nearly independently of the diocesan structures.

to become more directly involved in the hierarchical structure of the Church, presently recognizable as a wholly male preserve.

The establishment of all-female structures is in fact the recent history of women in the Church. Hundreds of thousands of generous women have created their own means of organizing their service to the Church and their own internal and external organizational structures by which their service may be supported: schools, hospitals, and social service agencies founded by women's religious institutes. These organizations are a model for diaconal service to the Church, but not necessarily the model for the female diaconate. Women's internal organizational structures — for the most part religious orders and institutes, but secular institutes as well — may have fallen on hard times in the West, yet it seems clear that they are both inheritors of the old roles and precursors to some new roles of women in the Church. That is, they are both inheritors of and precursors to the ordained female diaconate. Furthermore, as they live their particular charisms, they have no intention of dying out.[264] (Religious institutes of women would probably not accept previously ordained members, or allow present members to be ordained, specifically because in so doing they could become tied to the diocesan structure and lose their distinctive charisms. However, the separatism such bespeaks is of the ancient tension between the monastery and the diocesan bishop, not between men and women. The next chapter picks up this point.)

The point of ordaining women to the permanent diaconate is to serve the whole Church. A separatist argument, whether supported by feminists or by Church authority, presumes that the current structure and governance of the Church is open only to men and inverts the question to one in which a female structure could become a world into itself, thereby excluding the transcendent and, ultimately, the very concept of Church. In some cases such a female view can be understood because of the cultural per-

---

[264]See, for example, Patricia Wittberg, S.C., *Pathways to Re-Creating Religious Communities* (New York: Paulist Press, 1996) and Patricia Wittberg, S.C., *Creating a Future for Religious Life: A Sociological Perspective* (New York: Paulist Press, 1991).

spective by which so much of Church teaching is colored, that is, the separatist feminist argument appears to be the mirror image of a "male" Church.

Yet the Christian fact of the dignity of all people, both male and female, is so striking and so presumptuous of equality in dignity before the Lord God of all that it begs to be clarified by all in the Church. The Church has begun to recognize cultural proscriptions against women and can in its wisdom continue to do so. Ordaining women to the permanent diaconate would serve the whole Church in supporting its essential mission, the proclamation of the Gospel of Jesus Christ, first and foremost in supporting the dignity of all persons. Beyond, the Church's very being argues on behalf of returning to a female diaconate as a matter of justice, both to those who would serve and they whom they would serve.

Ordained diaconal service by women will support the function and stability of the whole Church.

The functions of the Church are not restricted to orders, but orders solidify a particular two-sided relationship with the Church. By incorporating some of the women who perform diaconal service into the permanent diaconate, the Church will additionally support its function and stability.

Women ministers are not presently treated in a legal manner identical to clerics, although some of the law relative to religious seems developed from that concept. Even so, law relative to religious does not apply to seculars. The Church, in the interest of preserving its power and authority, should of necessity have the same authority over those lay persons performing diaconal ministry as it has over deacons performing diaconal ministry. The service of women in diaconal ministry without ordination presents a one-sided commitment that is neither good for the Church nor good for the women so ministering.

For the most part, it would seem that arguments against the ordination of women to the diaconate, particularly insofar as ordained diaconal service by women would support the functions and stability of the whole Church, serve as well as arguments against the permanent diaconate as an institution of the contemporary Church. That is, the suggestion that a female diaconate would be a sort of professional excess for the Church, which still sees as its major necessity (and rightly so) two functions of priesthood — priest as confector of the Eucharist and priest as forgiver of sins — is specious unless it applies to the permanent diaconate in general. The growing Church, more and more bereft of priests, more and more dependent upon lay ministers for catechesis, has called for and needs the permanent diaconate.[265] Where in some parts of the word lay ministers are preferred over the possibility of women ordained to the permanent diaconate, the Church might appear to be preferring itself as a congregationalist organization. That is, the preference of the nonordained lay minister over a woman deacon effectively presents a preference for no juridical authority over, or sacramental power on behalf of, the community by the bishop. Such preference (by default) risks, for example, the transmutation of base communities from Church-oriented groups tied to the diocesan bishop to politically oriented groups tied to local issues. Further, where the sacraments of baptism and marriage are concerned, there comes a disjointedness when the catechist — male or female — cannot ordinarily solemnly celebrate or witness the sacrament for which he or she has prepared the candidates. The Church expressed these reasons for the restoration of the permanent diaconate after Vatican II;[266] such are additional reasons for the restoration of the permanent diaconate for women now.

For there to be stability in an organization there must also be clearly defined function. The Church recognizes this well, but in relatively recent times the understanding of the Church's multiple needs for ordained service have been conflated to be answered by priesthood. To continue to expand the functions contained in ordained service once again, drawing on the understanding of diaconate in *Lumen Gentium* and since then, and to recognize that

---

[265] Decree on the Church's Missionary Activity, *Ad Gentes*, 16, 17 (December 7, 1995), in Flannery, *Vatican Council II*, 832–83.
[266] Ibid.

the particular callings of women to service ought equally be represented by the service of the word and sacrament as deacon, would
be to continue in the tradition of hierarchical structure. Equally,
such would simultaneously expand the hierarchical structure to
include more people as ordained ministers, concurrently allowing
for many more people to be ministered to.

The organizational structure of the Church would suffer if the
inclusion of women in clearly defined ministries, and the solidifi-
cation of the functions of those ministries, each created additional
layers of bureaucracy. This does not seem to have been the case
with the restoration of the permanent diaconate for men. The
intent of ordaining women deacons would be not so much to
expand to a participatory democracy as to expand to a Church
that would share its sacramental presence more widely. Ordaining women deacons would strengthen certain existing service and
more clearly tie it to the whole Church, while expanding the
presence of ordained ministers in the Church.

When the faithful gather without leaders the faithful find little
recognition. Hence the various experiments alluded to earlier,
from the base communities of Latin America to the underground
women's experiments of the United States, can do more to separate than join their members to what the whole Church is doing
because sacrament is often in danger of being replaced both by
political action and by nonsacramental (and nonliturgical) ceremony. The coming together of persons in these circumstances risks
becoming a political, not a religious statement. Nonsacramental
ceremony does not in itself join the congregation to the Church,
and in the case of underground women's experiments the very
celebration of sacrament separates rather than joins the celebrating community to the whole Church. There is separation rather
than joining because there is *de facto* lack of intent to do as the
whole Church does, which is restrict celebration of sacrament ordinarily to those ordained and extraordinarily to those persons
so delegated by the bishop, within the limitations already noted.
Similarly, if the base communities had ordained leaders, leaders
unquestionably from the community, but acting truly in service

to it (rather than risk being in service to a political or ideological cause) the union with the whole Church would be complete and would better serve the political action that in many areas is necessary to support the work of the Church.[267] As it is, the work of these groups risks invasion by other activities, other agenda, other aims and goals. Both the sacramental nature of these local base communities and the nature of their sacraments can be called into question, if the intention of their union is not primarily as witness to Christ in union with the whole Church, but as Christians organized solely to provide support for another cause.

It is entirely possible that an overbureaucratization in the Church has of its nature created the need for smaller groups whose similarities are external to their religious commitment. Opponents of too much structure, including those who argue against any ordained clergy at all within the Church, recall the principle of subsidiarity first enunciated in *Quadragesimo Anno* (1931), an antibureaucratic concept that argues against the need for maintaining responsibility for anything within an organization at the highest possible level.[268] But, applied to ministry and argued in the reverse, subsidiarity could by extension come to mean literally the priesthood of all believers, a form of congregationalism. One might argue on behalf of women's ordination to both priesthood and diaconate from this standpoint, noting that since the women of the Church (most often women religious) are most often at the lowest level of intercession and at the most direct level of interaction with the People of God, it is they to whom the juridical and sacramental powers of ordained ministry ought most logically be given and given quickly, lest the concept of a sacramental Church be lost all together. Yet the opposite argument would maintain that women cannot perform the functions of priest (given the arguments of *Inter Insigniores* and *Ordinatio Sacerdotalis*), and therefore the juridical and sacramental powers

---

[267]This exposition of theory cannot overlook the fact that many poor basic Christian communities that do not have ordained leaders live in concert with the Church.

[268]See, for example, John Kelley, "Subsidiarity and Social Renewal," *African Ecclesiastical Review* 24 (August 1982): 200–208.

of priesthood must be the most restricted of all the complementary powers of the Church. Such is an argument that distinguishes
priesthood from the diaconate, not one that eliminates women
from the permanent diaconate. Further, it is Church authority,
not the People of God, which governs the notion of ordination
(somewhat in opposition to the more common view of the priest
being called from the community, despite how little this may cor-
respond to reality). In this sense, again, by withholding priesthood
from women Church authority argues on behalf of the diaconate
for women, as a functional and a structural need.

The hierarchical, or administrative, Church (Church authority), from the logic of *Quadragesimo Anno* can exist only to support
the whole Church (*subsidium*) (the People of God), as Dennis P.
McCann has pointed out.[269] When the Church can no longer
do so, that is, when the Church authority can no longer provide needed ministry, it is incumbent upon it to revert to earlier
methods of serving the people, even if those earlier methods have
fallen into disuse and even if those methods are misunderstood,
but only without risking fracture of the Church universal into
national churches.[270]

Ordained diaconal service by women should not replace unordained service by women.

While the Church has the jurisdiction and power to ordain women
to the diaconate, there remains a paradox in the call for orders.
The paradox is not relative to orders, but relative to service. It
would seem that because women have for the most part been
without power in modern times, women have had nothing to
lose and have consequently been able to effect more change

---

[269]Dennis P. McCann, *New Experiment in Democracy*, 137.

[270]"On the basis of the same principle [subsidiarity], the new Code entrusts either
to particular laws or to executive power whatever is not necessary for the unity of the
discipline of the universal Church so that appropriate provision is made for a healthy
'decentralization' while avoiding the danger of division into or the establishment of national churches." *Code of Canon Law* (Washington, D.C.: Canon Law Society of America,
1983), xxi.

in the Church than they might otherwise. Women, especially women not attached to religious institutes, have moved freely as a cadre of internal missionaries within and without the structure of the Church, independent of juridical relationships, specifically because they have not had the power or authority of orders. Without question, the charism of unordained service, mostly known through religious life, must perdure not because it is specifically female, but because it is a specific response to specific needs of the Church, needs that might not be equally served by individual clerics or clerical institutes. Therefore, as the Church needs to restore the service of ordained women, it must also retain the service of unordained women. Specifically, despite the possibility that apostolic religious life developed as an expression of diaconal service by women, it would be a great disservice to the Church to suddenly equate the female diaconate with apostolic religious life.

History is clear: women have been healers and women have been the proclaimers of the Word in deeds. Across different centuries, women have gathered in different ways: as deaconesses, as widows, as virgins; as canonesses and as nuns; as members of Third Orders; as apostolic religious. The most visible women of the Church in contemporary times have been sisters in apostolic institutes, many of whom are involved in services clearly (although not expressly) diaconal in nature. Since Vatican II, secular women in lay ministry have become increasingly visible. Neither is clearly bound to the service of the local Church or the diocesan bishop, who relates to individual women religious through their general superiors and to lay ministers even more remotely as an employer. Fewer women remain cloistered in monasteries. Yet all are obviously within the direct line of descent from deaconesses, canonesses, and mitered abbesses, just as are or were hermits, anchoresses, members of Third Orders and secular institutes, consecrated virgins, and seculars committed to the service of the Church.

There is no call or need for the Church to give up its careful distinction between vows and orders. It is the needs of the Church that have both required and allowed some members of women's apostolic institutes to, in one sense, substitute vows for orders, thereby weakening, or at least confusing, the evangelical presence of vowed women in the world. The effect of the conflation of so many historical vocations for women in the Church to membership in one or another apostolic institute of women creates an excess centrifugal force that could propel the eventual dissolution of some of these institutes. The financial exigencies of working in diaconal roles within the diocesan structure without the support of the larger Church both undermines the traditional institutions these same communities have built and has the potential of making these communities less attractive to new members because of lack of clarity of their mission or missions.[271] While individual members quite plainly serve in apostolic ministry that could be considered diaconal, as catechists, teachers, spiritual directors, and diocesan officers, they also serve as nurses, artists, librarians, secretaries, archivists, musicians, pharmacists, attorneys, managers, and consultants. The former might evidence the diaconal roots of religious life; the latter might reflect its monastic roots. The conflation of roles in apostolic institutes in one respect clouds their witness. The plethora of roles in these same institutes argues for the possibility of some women within them receiving diaconal orders as a means to strengthen and expand their ministries, should their respective institutes decide to include permanent deacons.

By including women — secular and religious — in the permanent diaconate, the distinctions between ordained and non-ordained commitment and service by women would be clarified. Further, the distinct discernments to ordained diaconal ministry and unordained ministry by seculars and religious alike would also be clarified. The result would likely be a clarification of several

---

[271]That is, as women religious gave up institutions that supported their independence, they became both increasingly parochialized (if they chose to work in diocesan structures) and increasingly less focused (especially where they work in individual secular occupations). Nygren and Ukeritis found relatively "low role clarity" among a large segment (59 percent) of apostolic religious. See David J. Nygren and Miriam D. Ukeritis, *The Future of Religious Orders in the United States*, 187–206.

distinct modes of being for women involved in ministry: secular lay ministers, religious lay ministers, secular ordained ministers, and religious ordained ministers. Expansion of and creation of new categories would allow women more opportunity to live their vocations of service without seeking ratification from religious communities. In fact, the need to retain membership as validation for ministry speaks to an intuitive understanding of at least one expression of apostolic religious life: it is fairly certain that the concept of the diocesan congregation is descended from the original female diaconate and related to the canoness institutes, and is similarly connected to the needs of the diocese as determined by the bishop.

By refusing the direct, ordained service of women and by concurrently seeming to consider membership in a religious community as tantamount to official approbation or certification for ministry that Church authority says would be strengthened by "the imposition of hands," the Church diminishes its rich tapestry of possibilities. For the most part, women who wish to serve the Church have only been able to do so by banding together in communities, which cooperatively provided housing and job placement through their own institutions or negotiated such placements with local bishops. Admitting women to the permanent diaconate would not change that appreciably. In fact, institutions owned and operated by women may still present the clearest opportunity for women's ministry in the future, with or without the possibility of ordained women deacons.[272]

Women are widely called to ministry in the Church.

There are two competing phenomena that make the picture of women in the Church confusing. There are no fewer women now, of any age, wishing to serve the Church than there ever were. But where do they go? The lack of clarity of mission and ministry on the part of many apostolic institutes, combined with various cultural factors, do not attract large numbers of women to them.

---

[272]Nygren and Ukeritis, *The Future of Religious Orders in the United States*, 236–39.

Hence, the competing phenomena: the dying out and breaking up of some active religious congregations, as women religious leave their convents to live intercongregationally or alone, and the coincidental surge of vocations to highly structured and traditional groups obscure the Church's need for both ordained and nonordained service by women.[273]

These apparently competing phenomena may not be so different after all. In some cases, the intercongregational setting is not unlike that of the Beguines, for the economic and emotional ties of women in these living situations are still primarily to the congregations through which they are publicly vowed, analogous in theory if not in fact to the personal property and lack of definite permanent commitment among the Beguines. Like the Beguines, these groups of women appear to escape most jurisdiction, either as regards work, which is often not connected to diocesan structures, or as regards living arrangements. In many respects, the modern "Beguinage" resembles a traditional convent.[274] There is clear and genuine interest of these women in the work and ministry of the Church. It is the Church that does not provide structure or security for women's ministry within the diocesan structure, and so women have provided their own security outside Church structures for each other. Intercongregational living brought about by common ministry, for example, in retreat houses or school convents, or in hospitals, shelters, or homes for children, regroups women according to a common mission, or a more congenial spirituality, or both. Such presents an extracongregational regrouping along the very traditional lines that originally led

---

[273]"Organizations and orders that appear strong have a dual formula of both a high cost of membership and high commitment rituals and practices to differentiate this group from any other. Until religious orders again understand the dynamics of commitment to prophetic and witness, they are not likely to see dramatic increases in membership." Nygren and Ukeritis, *The Future of Religious Orders in the United States,* 235.

[274]Commonly these work or living arrangements take on the various aspects of a women's community, often with implicit structures, procedures, and customs, which, while not fixed by common rule, are nearly identical to ministries or convents of a single group of women religious. In another sense, intercommunity living resembles the living arrangements of secular canonesses, who received a prebend from their work, but who did not necessarily commit their entire lives to the work or the community.

to the development of religious institutes. A countermovement of internal authority to regroup women religious according to their own congregational works and living arrangements, and in some cases to initiate new ministries that require common life and ministry, serves as recognition of the call of the Church to women to work in ordained ministry, often but not necessarily in the diocesan structure. The regrouping could mark a new commitment to the congregation's charism — its mission, ministry, community and prayer life — that might signal a rebirth. But the rebirth would be inserted into the charism of the given institute, not into the diocesan structure. As such, it would complement, not replace, the need for women in the permanent diaconate.

Ordained women deacons would support the Church's juridical and sacramental needs.

Very few women exercise jurisdiction within the structure of the hierarchical Church, although just as any other lay person they may "cooperate in the exercise of this power in accord with the norm of law."[275] Their real juridical authority, that is, the most obvious exercise of juridical authority by women, is restricted to within their own congregations and monasteries.[276]

---

[275]Canon 129.1. In accord with the prescriptions of law, those who have received sacred orders are capable of the power of governance, which exists in the Church by divine institution and is also called the power of jurisdiction.

2. Lay members of the Christian faithful can cooperate in the exercise of this power in accord with the norm of law.

[276]"In practice, unless approved proper law provides otherwise, all these superiors — cleric or lay — are competent according to the code to:

- formally establish internal divisions of the institute (c. 581), which can be provinces that are automatically public juridic persons (c. 638, para. 1);
- formally establish houses (c. 609, para. 1), which are automatically public juridic persons (c. 638, para. 1);
- suppress houses that have been formally established (c. 616, para. 1);
- represent the public juridic person (c. 118) in acts of administration regarding its ecclesiastical goods (cc. 634, para. 1, and 635, para. 1);
- formally establish and suppress novitiate houses (c. 647);
- admit members to temporary and to perpetual profession (cc. 656, 3* and 658);
- issue an indult of exclaustration for up to three years (c. 686, para. 1);

Not only women, but all lay persons are ordinarily restricted from exercising jurisdiction usually accorded clerics except by rescript. Church authority has made it clear that lay persons merely "cooperate," as opposed to "share," in the Church's exercise of power. In the development of the 1983 Code of Canon Law, the first approved construct of Canon 129, para. 2, stated that lay persons could share (*partem habere*), as opposed to cooperate (*cooperari*) in the exercise of power (*potestas*). However, the Church finally determined that "cooperate" was the proper word.

In her definitive study of the question of lay jurisdiction, canonist Elizabeth McDonough notes that, of the two prevailing schools of thought, the German is more restrictive, while "the Roman school of thought recognizes that the change in Canon 129 from *partem habere* to *cooperari* weakened the meaning of the text previously approved at the 1981 *Plenaria*. . . . Further, they say, the 1976 comments of the Congregation for the Doctrine of the Faith during the code revision process in response to a specific question about jurisdiction excluded laity from only those offices which exercise required orders."[277] McDonough includes an interesting footnote relative to the German school's use of the changes from *partem habere* to *cooperari* on the point of lay exercise of jurisdiction:

> However, the preponderance of comments as well as the decision on (then) canon 126 regarding laity and the exercise of jurisdiction at the 1981 *Plenaria* do not lend support to the German position. Although the reference to a power not rooted in sacred orders was deleted from the proposed norm, this was not understood in the discussions as excluding laity from exercising jurisdiction in some cases. The vote approving the wording of canon 129, which specifically included the possi-

---

- permit a member in temporary vows to depart from the institute (c. 688, para. 2); and
- issue a decree of dismissal, even for perpetually professed members (c. 699, para. 1)."

Elizabeth McDonough, "Jurisdiction Exercised by Non-Ordained Members in Religious Institutes," *Canon Law Society of America Proceedings* 58 (1996): 292–307, 306.

[277]McDonough, "Jurisdiction Exercised by Non-Ordained Members in Religious Institutes," 295.

bility of laity exercising jurisdiction, was an overwhelming 52 out of 61. See *Congregatio Plenaria,* 190–229. At that time the canon consisted of one paragraph and mentioned the ability of the supreme authority of the Church to grant laity a part in the exercise of *potestas regiminis.* The canon was separated into two paragraphs and the term *partem habere* was changed to *cooperari* after the 1982 version was submitted to the pope and a small commission of experts for final revisions. Cardinal Ratzinger, who had argued strongly for the German position in a pre-*Plenaria* written opinion, was a member of this final commission. With the exception of a comma, the final wording of para. 1 in (what eventually became) canon 129 is exactly the wording that Cardinal Ratzinger had previously proposed.[278]

The 1976 comments of the Congregation for the Doctrine of the Faith, solidified in 1980 and 1982 and ratified with the new code in 1983, followed two significant changes regarding the possible share in juridical power by laity that took place in and around the time of intense world and church discussion relative to women, including the preparation of the International Theological Commission's since-suppressed study on women deacons.[279] In 1972, Paul VI abolished tonsure and the four minor orders, making ordination to the diaconate the entrance to the clerical state; in 1975 he changed one stable part of papal elections, requiring that any person elected Pope must immediately be ordained bishop, thereby tying episcopal ordination to supreme power. (Previously, in 1945, Pius XII had stated that a lay person elected Pope would acquire "full and absolute jurisdiction" prior to entry to the clerical state.)[280] The restriction of jurisdiction and power to clerics, and supreme power to clerics who were bishops, would seem to be redundant except for the probability of women's ability in the

---

[278]McDonough refers to Cardinal Ratzinger's *animadversiones* and suggested text of December 22, 1980, in *Congregatio Plenaria,* 294, fn.4.

[279]See p. 45, above.

[280]McDonough, "Jurisdiction Exercised by Non-Ordained Members in Religious Institutes," 298–99, citing Paul VI, Apostolic constitution *Romano Pontifici Eligendo,* October 1, 1975, *Acta Apostolicae Sedis* 67 (1975): 609–45; *CLD* 8:133–69; and Pius XII, Apostolic constitution *Vacantis Apostolicae Sedis,* December 8, 1945, *Acta Apostolicae Sedis* 38 (1946): 65–99.

future to share in jurisdiction and power as they had in the past, especially but not only as clerics, either by simple admission to the clergy (through minor orders) or ordination to the diaconate, or election to a quasi-episcopal position (abbess), or, even, to the See of Peter.

There are significant restrictions to the sharing of power or the exercise of jurisdiction by women at present because all women are lay persons. It is *de facto,* if not expressly *de jure,* that lay persons cannot and do not generally cooperate fully in the exercise of the power of governance within the realm of the parish or diocese. The disadvantage is implicit in the lay status of women, and their consequent inability to assume ecclesiastical office ("any function constituted in a stable manner by divine or ecclesiastical law to be exercised for a spiritual purpose" [Canon 145]) where such office requires priesthood, for example, pastor or chaplain, or that requires clerical status, for example, single judge on a marriage tribunal.[281] Despite the increasing numbers of male and female lay chancellors, vice-chancellors, and marriage tribunal judges, the ordinary structures of Church governance rely, legally at least, on clerical status, if not priesthood.[282] What women do, therefore, is too often parallel and not juridically and sacramentally integrated within the work of the Church, either on the parish or the diocesan level, independent of whether they belong to religious congregations, orders, or institutes. The distinguishing of roles and abilities, between women (all lay persons) and clergy (all male), will, in accord with Church governance, continue. The line of demarcation will thicken as the increasing numbers of persons presently trained, or involved in training, for lay ministry, advance within the bureaucratic (although not the hierarchic) structures of the Church.

---

[281]Canon 150: "An office entailing the full care of souls, for whose fulfillment the exercise of the priestly order is required, cannot be validly conferred upon someone who has not yet received priestly ordination." (Interestingly, the rescript that allows for married priests refuses them the possibility of "care of souls," i.e., assignment as pastor, chaplain, administrator, etc.)

[282]See John Beal, "The Exercise of the Power of Governance by Lay People: State of the Question," *The Jurist* 55 (1995): 1–92, for an extensive discussion on this point.

A particular point of fraction between lay ministers, especially women ministers who would choose to be ordained if they could, and ordinary Church governance is the preaching of the homily within the celebration of the mass. Canon 766 allows that "lay persons can be admitted to preach in a Church or oratory if it is necessary in certain circumstances or if it is useful in particular cases according to the prescriptions of the conference of bishops and with due regard for can. 767 para. 1," which reserves the homily to a priest or a deacon.[283]

The key to this canon, and to this fraction, is the key to all Church law: "if it is necessary in certain circumstances or if it is useful in particular cases...."[284] Preaching a homily is confined to the ordained, but it is also a form of ministry. Ministry in its broadest sense is not restricted to the ordained, and in fact that ministry which is restricted to the ordained is in large part able to be performed "if it is necessary in certain circumstances or it is useful in particular cases" by nonordained persons, or by or-dained persons not of the required grade of orders.[285] Preaching is a specific point of concern, because the interpretation of doctrine, which it so naturally entails, includes the refusal of admission of

---

[283]Canon 767.1: "Among the forms of preaching the homily is preeminent; it is a part of the liturgy itself and is reserved to a priest or deacon." Readmission of women to the diaconate would *de facto* admit women to another level of teaching authority.

[284]The prior canon, Canon 765, notes that no one can preach to religious in their Church or oratory without permission of their own competent superior. It seems the as-sumption of Canon 766 is of preaching in a public Church or oratory: "Lay persons can be admitted to preach in a Church or oratory if it is useful in particular cases according to the prescriptions of the conference of bishops and with due regard for can. 767 para. 1." Canon 766.

[285]Military chaplains and missionaries, for example, routinely perform confirmations, and hospital workers routinely perform baptisms. By *Sacrae Religionis* (February 1, 1400) Boniface I allowed the Abbot of S. Osith in Essex to confer all orders up to and including the priesthood, although he revoked this permission at the insistence of the Bishop of London on juridical (not doctrinal) grounds with the bull *Apostolicae Sedis* (February 6, 1403). Similar jurisdictional authority was given by Martin V up to priesthood (*Gerentes ad vos*, November 16, 1427), and by Innocent VIII up to diaconate (*Exposcit*, April 9, 1489), and by others, apparently through the sixteenth century. See Piet Fransen, "Orders and Ordination," *Encyclopedia of Theology: The Concise Sacramentum Mundi* (New York: Seabury Press, 1975), 1122–48, 1136. A resistance to the ordination of women to the diaconate might be the implied possibility of their being granted faculties for the conferring of sacraments not within their grade of order, even if there is no implied possibility that women might be ordained to that same grade of order.

women to priesthood and the diaconate and, consequently, to
ordinary preaching faculties.

Ordaining women to the permanent diaconate would necessarily support the juridical and sacramental needs of the Church
precisely where most needed. Women's abilities to function within
the structure of the Church in the name of the Church *without*
involving an ontological discussion (or discrediting the iconic argument) relative to the ability of women to act *in persona Christi*,
support women's inclusion in the permanent diaconate as a means
of more fully supporting the Church's juridical and sacramental
needs in an ordinary, rather than extraordinary, manner.

The permanent diaconate is not a lay state. The Decree on
the Apostolate of Lay People notes that "the characteristic of
the lay state being a life led in the midst of the world and of
secular affairs, laymen are called by God to make of their apostolate, through the vigor of their Christian spirit, a leaven in the
world."[286] Secular and religious women who live lives of service
to the Church are distinguished from permanent deacons in that
their lives are such leaven in the world. The possibility of a permanent diaconate for women, both distinct from and conjoined with
religious life, gives women the possibility of being leaven in the
world *and* in the Hierarchy, as clerics. The restored permanent
diaconate is new to the Church, but it provides for the juridical and sacramental needs of the Church in an ordinary, not an
extraordinary manner, and as such provides for a necessity in a
way no other ministry can.[287] Including women would provide for
necessity even more.

---

[286]Decree on the Apostolate of Lay People, *Apostolicam Actuositatem* (November 18,
1995), in Flannery, *Vatican Council II*, 768.

[287]The 1994–95 national study on the permanent diaconate found that nearly half
of parish council members and about 43 percent of (mostly priest) supervisors of deacons
surveyed thought the ministries that deacons perform could be equally well-performed by
a lay person. This would by necessity include liturgical and sacramental ministries. See *A
National Study on the Permanent Diaconate of the Catholic Church in the United States, 1994–
1995* (Washington, D.C.: United States Catholic Conference, 1996), 41, 116. The rescript
for the Archdiocese of Anchorage, Alaska, requires that lay administrators of parishes
apply each time to the Archbishop or his delegate for permission to assist at a wedding.

The Church has begun to recognize the need to symbolize the service of women.

If the liturgy is symbolic of the daily mission and ministry of the Church, a sanctuary full of men creates a cognitive dissonance on the part of the worshiping community. Despite John Paul II's call to include women in altar service, and even though the interpretation of Canon 230 that admits any lay person to the function of lector or acolyte[288] this canon maintains that only men may be permanently installed to the ministries of lector and acolyte. That is, women may serve as acolytes or lectors, but may not be installed as such on a stable basis.[289] Hence, there is no liturgical function a woman may ordinarily fill.

The relatively recent recognition of the interpretation of the law allowing for women's altar service did not come without argument from conservative quarters, but more important than the proper translation of the canon was the ability of Church legislators to see the need for the service of women to be additionally symbolized by altar service in all the functions of acolyte.

That the ministry of women can be additionally symbolized by altar service as acolyte, in addition to service as lector, is significant in that acolytes are usually vested, either in alb or cassock and surplice. While there has never been any prohibition of women being so vested, there never seemed to be the need (with the exception of choir service), despite liturgical regulations that called for all ministers at the altar to at least wear an alb.[290] The ap-

---

[288]Canon 230.1 restricts installation as lector or acolyte to men; Canon 230.2 notes that any lay person can fulfill the function of lector by "temporary deputation"; Canon 230.3 states that any lay person can "supply" for the offices of lector or acolyte. As noted earlier, the point of discussion in the United States was whether *videlicet* was restrictive or merely demonstrative, whether it meant "namely" or "for example" in this paragraph, as follows: "Ubi Ecclesiae necessitas id suadeat, deficientibus ministris, possunt etiam laici, etsi non sint lectores vel acolythi, quaedam eorundem officia supplere, videlicet ministerium verbi exercere, precibus liturgicis praeesse, baptismum conferre atque sacram Communionem distribuere, iuxta iuris praescripta."

[289]*Ministeria Quaedam* of Paul VI eliminated the minor orders, leaving only the installed ranks of lector and acolyte. Typically, only persons in preparation for priesthood are permanently installed as lectors or acolytes, but the provision for permanent installation would in and of itself argue for more than such a temporary deputation.

[290]See the "General Instruction of the Roman Missal," no. 298: "The vestment com-

parent dropping of this requirement of proper vesting for those
who distribute communion and hence serve temporarily in the
ministry of acolyte, with the concurrent widespread inclusion of
women in the ministry of acolyte, was not repeated when females
were formally permitted to function as acolytes in the position of
server, lucifer, thurifer, crucifer, etc. It would seem that for altar
servers vesting is maintained in part because primarily preadoles-
cent males and females serve thusly. Adult nonclerical men and
women, except cantors and choir members, are not routinely seen
vested. This may change, for while the Church is still not used
to seeing adult women serving at the altar wearing cassock and
surplice or alb, an entire generation is growing up with this as a
normal practice.[291]

The alb signifies ministry; altar service symbolizes ministry. The
ministry of women, so symbolized by altar service, needs a realistic basis for its signs. Echoes of the distinctions between styles of
the Petrine ministry are felt at every level of Church governance,
and whether the default is on the communal-collegial-ecclesial
style of governance, or on the juridical-collaborative-political
style of governance, matters deeply in relation to the ministry
of women and of men who are not clerics.[292] The communal-
collegial-ecclesial style of governance allows for a less restrictive
understanding of "necessity" in the deputation of lay persons
to perform certain sacramental or other public acts (such as
preaching) that are ordinarily juridically restricted to clerics;
the juridical-collaborative-political style of governance allows for
a more restrictive understanding, more solidly withholding the

---

mon to ministers at every rank is the alb, tied at the waist with a cincture, unless it is
made to fit without a cincture," and no. 301: "Ministers below the order of deacon may
wear the alb." *The Roman Missal, The Sacramentary* (New York: Catholic Book Publishing
Co., 1985), 46*.

[291] Specifically, female altar servers. More formal churches still restrict distribution of
communion to men wearing albs or cassock and surplice, and they are always clerics or
seminarians, although one (St. Patrick's Cathedral in New York) now permits women
religious wearing habits to distribute communion. Such reflects on the need for both
preparation and some sort of "vesting" appropriate to the action.

[292] For a discussion of the varied forms of governance and their consequences, see
Phyllis Zagano and Terrence W. Tilley, eds., *The Exercise of the Primacy: Continuing the
Dialogue* (New York: Crossroad, 1998).

power of office to the ordained, and presenting a seeming distaste for the principles of subsidiarity. Curiously, the latter argues more on behalf of the ordination of women to the diaconate than the former.

Church authority recognizes the need for women's shared authority and responsibility.

All ministers are or ought to be in communal relationship with their bishop or major superior; all ministry therefore is rendered cooperative rather than representational, i.e., a reflection of the first type of Church governance (communal-collegial-ecclesial) rather than the second (juridical-collaborative-political). If ministry is truly a cooperative[293] rather than a hierarchical enterprise in which women can share power, then the argument for women to be ordained to service is even stronger despite the growing recognition of the laity's ability to cooperate in governance.[294] Even those American bishops known as the most conservative in the Church seem to recognize that women are eligible to cooperate in the power of governance, both as lay persons and — were it to come about — as clerics. For example, when asked if he saw the diaconate as a separate ministry in the service of the bishop for the Church rather than as a step toward the priesthood, and about the possibility of women deacons, Bernard Cardinal Law of Boston answered:

> Diaconate is an order distinct from priesthood and distinct from the order of Bishop but yet those sacred orders have been seen together. We have restored the permanent diaconate. Again, if

---

[293]Canon 129.2: "Lay members of the Christian faithful can cooperate in the exercise of this power [the power of governance] in accord with the norm of law."

[294]See John Beal, "Jurisdiction by the Laity," *The Jurist* 55 (1995): 1–92 and, as above, McDonough "Jurisdiction Exercised by Non-Ordained Members in Religious Orders," 292–307 and, to a lesser degree, Ladislas Orsy, "Lay Persons in Church Governance? A Disputed Question," *America* 174, no. 11 (April 6, 1996): 10. Orsy also translates two documents that show governance by abbesses: an 1858 document signed by the Abbess of Las Huelgas in Spain granting faculties to a priest, and 1708 and 1709 documents that recognize the jurisdiction of the Abbess of Castellana in Italy over the clergy of her territory. Pius IX abolished the juridical privileges of the Abbess of Las Huelgas, Spain, in 1873, which abolition nevertheless admits further to their validity.

I'm not mistaken, the document on the ordination of women from the Sacred Congregation for the Doctrine of the Faith indicated that the matter of diaconate needed study. So, I think that study needs to proceed.

Again, if the case can be made for seeing that [the diaconate] as distinct from the priesthood, then fine. Then we should move towards that if that is in fact the result of the study backed by the authority of the Church's decision.[295]

As the context makes clear, "that" is the ordination of women to the diaconate. Cardinal Law's restrictions and understandings actually echo those of bishops centuries earlier who insisted that women ordained to the diaconate be able to work with the presbyters, who were apparently all male, and on behalf of their bishops. That is, the notion of collaboration was prior to and a requirement for actual ministry; those who could not collaborate were not to be ordained.[296]

Diocesan guidelines ensure that those to be ordained are those who can cooperate in mission and ministry, although a prior problem to the reincorporation of women into the clergy as deacons is presented by a changing understanding of the role of the deacon. There are varying degrees of ministerial relations between priests and permanent deacons. Among deacons, there seems to be a division between deacons who see themselves as ordained to altar service and those who see themselves as ordained to service to the community. The problems of the permanent deacon in the Church in America will not be solved here, in part because it is the immediate duty of the whole Church to make a clear decision as to whether it wants permanent deacons to be clerics in orders, or it wants deacons to be specially deputized and "installed" laity extraordinarily authorized to preach, witness marriages, perform baptisms, and serve as judges. Matters are further

---

[295]Interview, November 30, 1987.

[296]The woman deacon "ought to be a good minister, sober, in communication with the presbyters, not desirous of monetary gain, nor given to much wine, so that she might be able to keep watch through the night in ministry and to do whatever good deeds might be asked [of her], for these are the first gifts of the Lord." *Apostolic Canons of the Church*, Canon 21.

confused when deacons are referred to as "lay deacons." While permanent deacons are clerics in orders, they are not, for the most part, in the "clergy," or ordinarily considered as part of the bishop's "household," except perfunctorily.[297]

The question then arises whether the Church in restoring the permanent diaconate is raising up a super-laity that can be given ordinary faculties for what the laity can extraordinarily do. Given that most instances of such extraordinary deputation to women is to women religious, the addition of clerical orders would seem to be superlative. As noted above, with the exception of serving as a single judge, any lay person may be juridically — usually temporarily in single cases — authorized to perform many of the functions of deacon, especially to baptize and to witness marriages.[298] Still, only clerics may serve as a single judge in "a trial of first instance."[299]

While it was not always the case, the ordinary way in which men now enter the clerical state is through ordination to the diaconate.[300] (To be clear: women are restricted from the clerical state because it is ordinarily entered through ordination to the diaconate, not because orders are necessarily intrinsic to the cler-

---

[297]Diocesan newspapers, for example, where they publish the necrology of diocesan clerics, include deacons along with priests and bishops.

[298]The Archdiocese of Anchorage first obtained a five-year renewable rescript from Rome, January 3, 1990, which it has used about a dozen times since then, mostly for women religious running rural parishes as pastoral administrators, although two other lay persons have been permitted to preside at weddings.

[299]Canon 1425.4: "If it happens that a collegiate tribunal cannot be established for a trial of first instance, the conference of bishops can permit the bishop to entrust cases to a single clerical judge as long as the impossibility of establishing a college perdures; he is to be a cleric and is to employ an assessor and an auditor where possible."

[300]Canon 266.1: "A person becomes a cleric through the reception of diaconate and is incardinated into the particular church or personal prelature for whose service he has been advanced." The history of the clerical state, and by implication the diaconate, finds it fraught with political overtones. Briefly: the concept of a restored diaconate was overcome in the Council of Trent, mainly because council reformers wished to do away with the practice of Church benefices for those who entered into minor orders only for political or financial gain. Members of the papal diplomatic corps, however, were ordained deacons routinely until 1870, when the creation of the Papal State made such unnecessary. See Norbert Brockman, *Ordained to Service: A Theology of the Permanent Diaconate* (Hicksville, N.Y.: Exposition Press, 1976), 30–31. Brockman on this point cites Edward R. Hardy, "Deacons in History and Practice," in *The Diaconate Now*, ed. Richard T. Nolan (Washington, D.C.: Corpus, 1968), 26–34.

ical state.) It would take a derogation from the law for a bishop now to admit a woman to the clerical state without ordination and, implicitly, to his "household." The fact that any lay person can be extraordinarily but routinely granted faculties for baptism and for marriage, allowing clerical service with neither clerical status nor the grace of orders, suggests a solution, but is not a solution in itself. The increasing necessity for rescripts for such extraordinary faculties points all the more to the need for ordained women deacons, as Church authority continues to recognize the need for women's sharing — as well as cooperating in — authority and power.

Ordaining women deacons would more clearly distinguish the diaconate.

It would seem that the Church would wish to regularize the ministry of women, that is, to make some accommodation to the growing numbers of women who could better serve the Church in their present positions if they were clerics. As the Church continues to understand the diaconate within the modern context, it must answer questions on how the diaconate is needed to serve it. Canon law dictates that all Christians "have become sharers in Christ's priestly, prophetic and royal office in their own manner,"[301] so it would follow that in this sense deacons share in the priestly office without necessarily acting *in persona Christi*. Deacons also juridically share in the authority of the bishop and act by his leave in the name of the Church through the receipt and exercise of faculties.

The threefold ministry of the deacon as synthesized by the Second Vatican Council is of the liturgy, of the word, and of charity. So it is the duty of the deacon — male or female — to proclaim the Gospel, be both homilist and catechist, assist both bishops

---

[301]Canon 204.1: "The Christian faithful are those who, inasmuch as they have been incorporated in Christ through baptism, have been constituted as the People of God; for this reason, since they have become sharers in Christ's priestly, prophetic and royal office in their own manner, they are called to exercise the mission which God has entrusted to the Church to fulfill in the world, in accord with the condition proper to each one."

and priests at liturgical celebrations, administer baptism, witness marriages, provide pastoral care to the sick, celebrate the liturgy of the hours, minister sacramentals and obsequies (funeral and burial rites), and serve the mission of charity through pastoral or diocesan ministry.[302]

The questions about the permanent diaconate in general are at the heart of the notion of ordaining women to it. But the Church in its wisdom raised up a permanent diaconate that includes all the roles in which women have served and do serve today. *Lumen Gentium* is quite clear on the matter:

> At a lower level of the hierarchy are to be found deacons, who receive the imposition of hands "not unto the priesthood, but unto the ministry." For, strengthened by sacramental grace, they are dedicated to the People of God, in conjunction with the bishop and his body of priests, in the service of the liturgy, of the Gospel, and of works of charity.[303]

It is precisely because the whole Church believes that the deacon is "strengthened by sacramental grace" that the deacon is able to be "dedicated to the People of God, in conjunction with the bishop and his body of priests, in the service of the liturgy, of the Gospel, and of works of charity." Because Church authority teaches it does not have the authority to ordain women to priesthood, and because of the cultural acceptance of the iconic argument, the woman deacon would be even more clearly distinguished from priests and bishops by virtue of gender. The symbolic addition

---

[302]Congregation for Catholic Education and Congregation for the Clergy, *Basic Norms for the Formation of Permanent Deacons and Directory for the Ministry and Life of Permanent Deacons* (Washington, D.C.: United States Catholic Conference, 1998), 88–108.

[303]*Lumen Gentium*, no. 29, which continues: "It pertains to the office of a deacon, in so far as it may be assigned to him by the competent authority, to administer Baptism solemnly, to be custodian and distributor of the Eucharist, in the name of the Church, to assist at and to bless marriages, to bring Viaticum to the dying, to read the sacred scripture to the faithful, to instruct and exhort the people, to preside over the worship and the prayer of the faithful, to administer sacramentals, and to officiate at funeral and burial services. Dedicated to works of charity and functions of administration, deacons should recall the admonition of St. Polycarp: 'Let them be merciful, and zealous, and let them walk according to the truth of the Lord, who became the servant of all.'" The quote from St. Polycarp is from *Ad Phil.* 5, 2. The internal quote in the text above is from *Constitutions of the Egyptian Church, III.*

of women in formal liturgy would clearly serve both to recognize their ministerial service and to represent all women as worthy of being near sacred things. Any view of diaconate as an incomplete priesthood, which Louis Boyer, among others, calls a misunderstanding of both priesthood and diaconate,[304] would dissolve for those who hold to Church teaching on priestly orders.

It is clear that all ministry by women in the Church is presently lay ministry, and in dioceses where necessity has outstripped personnel there is a tremendous amount of lay ministry performed by generous persons engaged in ongoing formation and education as they are called from the community of believers to minister to its members. Calls to better organize and recognize lay ministry generally focus on the need for clear relationships with the Church,[305] but since the predominance of individuals engaged in lay ministry is female, their ordination to the diaconate would allow for permanence on terms already determined by Church authority. Calls for a semi-"clericalization" short of ordination reflect the growing professionalism of lay ministry, but do not address the value of the charism of orders and seem to be developed as an alternative to the restoration of the ordained female diaconate.[306] Such an alternative seems to have been suggested in a draft of the National Conference of Catholic Bishops' pastoral on women ("Partners in the Mystery of Redemption: A Pastoral Response to Women's Concerns for Church and Society"), which was eventually abandoned:

> Women serving in pastoral ministry accomplish, by virtue of
> some other title or commission, many of the functions per-

---

[304]Louis Boyer, *Woman in the Church*, trans. Marilyn Teichert (San Francisco: Ignatius Press, 1979), 82.

[305]"The church seems increasingly prepared to count on lay persons to fill and carry out formal positions of ministry and needs to provide a clear place for them." Philip J. Murnion and David DeLambo, *Parishes and Parish Ministry: A Study of Parish Lay Ministry* (New York: National Pastoral Life Center, 1999), 68.

[306]"If, however, 'clericalization' connotes the establishment of a new class or formal group in the church, one that is distinct from the rest of the body of the laity and removes the lay ministers from their lay status, then there may actually be reason to think that there is not enough of this. Some clear and distinct structure may be precisely what is needed." Murnion and Delambo, *Parishes and Parish Ministry*, 68.

formed by ordained deacons and are capable of accomplishing all of them. The question of being formally *installed* in the permanent diaconate arises quite naturally, and pastoral reasons prompt its evaluation.[307]

What is problematic about this formulation is that in it either the diaconate is viewed as a lay ministry to which individuals may be installed (such as acolytes or lectors), or women can *only* be "installed" into a separate female diaconal ministry, distinct from the ordained (male) diaconate, perhaps reflecting and solidifying a distinction between deacons and deaconesses. These matters were addressed earlier (Are women so different from men that they are unable to receive all the sacraments? Does the sacrament of orders *per se* configure the individual to Christ so that the individual must equally be configured to Christ in a symbolic way [an internal iconic argument]? Does any historical notion of deaconess deny a contemporary female diaconate?). Since the argument from authority does not apply to the diaconate, the question seems only to be whether the iconic argument extends to the diaconate. That is, are women presently "unordainable" iconically, or merely legally?[308]

If, for the benefit of the Church, the diaconate ought be more clearly distinguished from both lay ministry and priesthood, then it would seem that inclusion of women in the permanent diaconate would show the Church's recognition of the ability of women as well as men to be permanently configured through orders to Christ in a ministry of service so distinct as to serve in and of itself as

---

[307]Emphasis mine. National Conference of Catholic Bishops, "Partners in the Mystery of Redemption: A Pastoral Response to Women's Concerns for Church and Society," April 1988 draft, p. 117, para. 220.

[308]The Canon Law Society of America committee found that the restriction of diaconal ordination to males is a "merely ecclesiastical law" (Canon 11). See *The Canonical Implications of Ordaining Women to the Permanent Diaconate* (Washington, D.C.: Canon Law Society of America, 1995), 38. Therefore, apparently the restriction against women deacons can be overcome, as per Canon 19: "Unless it is a penal matter, if an express prescription of universal or particular law or a custom is lacking in some particular matter, the case is to be decided in light of laws passed in similar circumstances, the general principles of law observed with canonical equity, the jurisprudence and praxis of the Roman Curia, and the common and constant opinion of learned persons."

exemplar of the sacrament of orders for those who act *in nomine Christi* without necessarily needing to be able to act *in persona Christi* as the Church currently understands it.

Beyond the enhanced distinction of the diaconate with the inclusion of women, ordination would serve to formalize the relations with the diocesan bishop called for by proponents of lay ministry beyond any means presently undertaken.[309]

Again, the Church distinguishes the diaconate from other ministries. The Decree on the Church's Missionary Activity calls for ordination to support the needs recognized by lay ministers worldwide:

> It would help those men who carry out the ministry of a deacon — preaching the word of God as catechists, governing scattered Christian communities in the name of the bishop or parish priest, or exercising charity in the performance of social or charitable works — if they were to be strengthened by the imposition of hands which has come down from the apostles. They would be more closely bound to the altar and their ministry would be made more fruitful through the sacramental grace of the diaconate.[310]

The Church at large recognizes its authority to ordain women deacons.

Given the recognition that the female diaconate would distinguish both the diaconate and lay ministry, there are two points to consider. First, does the Church truly want to integrate and incorporate the ministry of women in a more formal manner? And, if it does, how shall it proceed?

---

[309]The Auxiliaries of the Apostolate comprise three thousand women in three hundred dioceses worldwide, individually called to permanent service by the local ordinary. Even so, they have no claim to health care or employment — no prebend — from the dioceses to which they belong. Founded after World War I by Cardinal Mercier, Archbishop of Malines, they have a formation center at Lourdes and form their members there when formation is not available within a given diocese. Barbara Davies, one of their members, cites the same passages used to argue for women deacons as explanation of their vocation. See Barbara Davis, "Auxiliary of the Apostolate: What on Earth...?" *Clergy Review* 63 (1978): 6–19. There are very few members (perhaps seven) in the United States.

[310]Decree on the Church's Missionary Activity, *Ad Gentes*, no. 16, in Flannery, *Vatican Council II*, 833.

One response might find that ordination is unnecessary. Women already in the service of the Church could be extraordinarily granted faculties to serve in many diaconal roles — juridical and sacramental — immediately on a permanent basis, instead of on a case-by-case basis. This is not the solution for those who see the ordained deacon participating in apostolic ministry and ministering *in nomine Christi*. While a permanent contractual extraordinary granting of faculties would create and retain a formal relationship between the bishop and the minister, it avoids the recognition of the sacramental grace of orders and risks the creation of a professional class of ministers neither ordained nor fully lay.

Given that those ordained would be required to ascribe to Church teaching on the manner of ordination to priesthood and episcopacy, it would seem that the creation of a professional class of highly trained lay ministers not bound in obedience to a bishop would be precisely what Church authority would seek to avoid.

The teaching Church has demonstrated its authority over the priestly orders with *Inter Insigniores* and *Ordinatio Sacerdotalis*. Similarly, the teaching Church holds authority over diaconal orders, and scholarly societies as well as episcopal and national conferences have called for the teaching Church to exercise that authority to allow for the return to the practice of ordaining women deacons.

The Catholic Theological Society of America in 1971 issued a report calling for the Church to be open to ordaining women deacons.[311] Indeed, as early as 1972 the International Theological Commission initiated a study of the role of deaconesses in the future of the Church,[312] which study is probably the suppressed study of the International Theological Commission referred to by Peter Hebblethwaite in *Paul VI* and in which Cipriano Vagaggini prob-

---

[311] Sue Cribari, "Theologians' recommendation: 'Be Open to Women Deacons'" *National Catholic Reporter*, March 5, 1971, 1, 14. The document also called for granting deacons the juridical and sacramental authority to hear confessions in conjunction with ministry to the sick.

[312] *Crux*, August 4, 1972, as cited in Brockman, *Ordained to Service*, 56.

ably had a hand.[313] The Joint Synod of the Dioceses of the Federal Republic of Germany asked Paul VI to examine the question in 1975; their request was repeated in 1981 and 1987.[314] When directly asked about the possibility of women deacons during his trip to New York in 1988, Joseph Cardinal Ratzinger responded that "it is under study."[315] Drafts of a document on women issued by the bishops of the United States in 1988 and 1990 each asked for the inclusion of women in the permanent diaconate; two later drafts, in 1991 and 1992, urged further study on the matter.[316] The following year, the National Association of Permanent Diaconate Directors asked the U.S. Catholic bishops to again ask Rome to investigate the possibility of women deacons.[317]

According to a statement by the then-secretary of the Congregation for the Clergy, Archbishop Crescenzio Sepe, to an international gathering of permanent diaconate directors at Bressanone, Italy, in October 1997, the Vatican (probably the Congregation for the Doctrine of the Faith, which Cardinal Ratzinger

---

[313]Vagaggini's article "L'ordinazione della diaconesse nella tradizione grèca e bizantina," *Orientalia Christiana Periodica* 40 (1974): 146–89, in which he pointed out that women deacons were ordained by the bishop in the presence of the presbyterate and within the sanctuary by the imposition of hands (151), may flow from that research. The suppression of the study is noted in Peter Hebblethwaite, *Paul VI: The First Modern Pope* (New York and Mahwah, N.J.: Paulist Press, 1993), 640. Members of the Commission are listed in Michael Sharkey, ed., *International Theological Commission: Texts and Documents 1969–1985* (San Francisco: Ignatius Press, 1989): 327–28. The Commission included Joseph Ratzinger, Louis Boyer, Yves Congar, O.P., and Americans Barnabas Ahern, C.P., and Walter Burghardt, S.J.

[314]*Gemeinsame Synode der Bistümer in der Bundesrepublik Deutschland, Offizielle Gesamtausgabe I* (Freiburg: Herder, 1976), 634, *votum* 7.1,3, as cited in Canon Law Society of America, *The Canonical Implications of Ordaining Women to the Permanent Diaconate* (Washington, D.C.: Canon Law Society of America, 1995), 4, 39.

[315]Cardinal Ratzinger lectured at St. Peter's Lutheran Church in New York on January 27, 1988. See Peter Steinfels, "Cardinal Is Seen as Kind, If Firm, Monitor of Faith," *New York Times*, February 1, 1988, A20.

[316]National Conference of Catholic Bishops Ad hoc Committee for a Pastoral Response to Women's Concerns, "Partners in the Mystery of Redemption: First Draft of a Pastoral Response to Women's Concerns for Church and Society," *Origins* 17, no. 45 (April 21, 1988): 781; "One in Christ Jesus: A Pastoral Response to the Concerns of Women for Church and Society," *Origins* 19, no. 44 (April 5, 1990): 730; "Called to Be One in Christ Jesus," *Origins* 21, no. 46 (April 23, 1992): 772; and "One in Christ Jesus," *Origins* 22, no. 13 (September 19, 1992): 235.

[317]Resolution of the National Association of Permanent Diaconate Directors of America, Orlando, Fla., April 23, 1993.

heads) was to issue a response to the question of women deacons "soon."[318]

Soundings from Rome, however, do not bode well for those who expect Church discipline to return to the practice of ordaining women deacons soon. As recently as the spring of 1999, Darío Cardinal Castrillón Hoyos, prefect of the Congregation for the Clergy, said that ordaining women would have to be tied to tradition, and "'the most serious studies at this point have clarified one thing' — the word 'deacon' in the New Testament and the description of what tasks women deacons performed is not the same as the church's understanding of an ordained deacon today."[319] (Despite this comment, as has been demonstrated, the work deaconess involved most, if not all, the functions of deacon. Further, the Church's "understanding of an ordained deacon today" is not identical to what men deacons did either.)

Cardinal Ratzinger, in his reply to the results of the Dialogue for Austria, made an administrative rather than substantive observation about their recent call for women deacons:

Theme 7, Recommendation 3

In this recommendation the Austrian bishops' conference is asked to intervene for the introduction of the permanent diaconate for women. In this question it is necessary to observe the proper conversational protocol. It must also be observed that the church law according to which only a baptized man can receive a valid ordination has important doctrinal implications (*Catechism of the Catholic Church* 1576; Canon 1024).[320]

---

[318]Telephone interview, John Pistone, Executive Director, National Conference of Catholic Bishops/United States Catholic Conference Committee on the Diaconate, June 15, 1998.

[319]"Cardinal Says Ordination of Women Deacons Unlikely," *National Catholic Reporter,* April 9, 1999, 9. The Colombian Cardinal noted there were many other services women could provide the Church that did not involve ordination. His statement is apparently echoed in the 1999 working document of the International Theological Commission.

[320]"Ratzinger's Reply to the Dialogue for Austria," *National Catholic Reporter,* April 9, 1999, 7, *National Catholic Reporter* translation. No. 1576 of the *Catechism of the Catholic Church* regards who may administer Holy Orders. More probably, no. 1577 is meant: "'Only a baptized man (*vir*) validly receives sacramental ordination.' The Lord Jesus chose men (*vir*) to form the college of the twelve apostles, and the apostles did the same when they chose collaborators to succeed them in their ministry. The college of bishops, with whom

The use of law to determine sacramental validity, the "important doctrinal implications," avoids both the ontological and the historical recognitions of the ability of women to serve as deacons and be ordained to that service.

Summary

Belief in the charism of orders supports the need to include women among the ordained. Ordained diaconal service by women responds to the needs of the whole Church, because it will support the function and stability of the whole Church. But ordained diaconal service by women should not replace unordained service by women. Women are widely called to ministry in the Church, and ordained women deacons would support the Church's juridical and sacramental needs. The Church has begun to recognize the need to symbolize the service of women, and Church authority recognizes the need for women's shared authority and responsibility. Ordaining women deacons would more clearly distinguish the diaconate. The Church at large recognizes its authority to ordain women deacons. Therefore, the ordained ministry of service by women is necessary to the Church, that is, to both the People of God and the Hierarchy.

---

priests are united in the priesthood, makes the college of the twelve an ever-present and ever-active reality until Christ's return. The Church recognizes herself to be bound by this choice made by the Lord himself. For this reason the ordination of women is not possible" (citing Canon 1024; Mark 3:14–19; Luke 6:12–16; 1 Tim. 3:1–13; 2 Tim. 1:6; Titus 1:5–9; St. Clement of Rome, *Ad Cor.* 42,4; 44,3: PG 1, 292–93; 300). Note that only bishops and priests are mentioned.

PART THREE

CONCLUSIONS

The ordination of women to the diaconate is possible.

The prior chapters lead ineluctably to the conclusion that the ordination of women to the diaconate is possible. In fact, Church authority already implicitly recognizes the fact of validly ordained women deacons.

The ordination of women is a matter of ecumenical interest.

The Churches of the East separated "either because of the dispute over the dogmatic formulae of the Councils of Ephesus and Chalcedon, or later by the dissolving of ecclesial communion between the Eastern Patriarchates and the Roman See."[321] However, their apostolic succession and sacrament of orders is accepted by the Catholic Church, as delineated by the Decree on Ecumenism, *Unitatis Redintegratio*:

> These Churches, although separated from us, yet possess true sacraments, above all — by apostolic succession — the priesthood and the Eucharist, whereby they are still joined to us in closest intimacy. Therefore some worship in common (*communicatio in sacris*), given suitable circumstances and the approval of Church authority, is not merely possible, but encouraged.[322]

These Churches include the several particular local Churches separated around the time of Chalcedon (Armenian, Syrian, Coptic,

---

[321]*Unitatis Redintegratio*, in *Vatican Council II: The Conciliar and Post Conciliar Documents*, ed. Austin Flannery, O.P. (Wilmington, Del.: Scholarly Resources, 1975), 463.

[322]Ibid., 465.

Malankara, and Ethiopian) and the several Churches separated in 1054 (i.e., Greek, Russian). The sacraments of each are recognized by the Decree on Ecumenism of the Second Vatican Council. As regards baptism: "There can be no doubt cast upon the validity of baptism as conferred among the separated Eastern Christians."[323] As regards Eucharist, the Decree on Ecumenism, no. 40, states that common recognition of apostolic succession

> offers ecclesiological and sacramental grounds for allowing and even encouraging some sharing in liturgical worship — even eucharistic — with these churches 'given suitable circumstances and the approval of church authority' (Decree on Ecumenism, no. 15).[324]

What is of particular import here is the Church's acceptance of the apostolic succession, hence of the validity of the sacrament of orders, of the Eastern Churches.

The Orthodox Churches have found that women can be ordained deacons.

Perhaps the most authoritative studies regarding the ordination of women in the Eastern Churches are two by Evangelos Theodorou: *Heroines of Love: Deaconesses through the Ages* (1949) and *The 'Ordination' or 'Appointment' of Deaconesses* (1954), and the work by Cipriano Vagaggini discussed earlier, "L'ordinazione delle diaconesse nella tradizione grèca e bizantina," published in 1974 in *Orientalia Christiana Periodica*.[325] Each scholar concludes that women received sacramental ordination to the diaconate.

In her recent comprehensive study of deaconesses in the Orthodox Churches, Kyriaki Karidoyanes FitzGerald notes that despite the decline of the order of woman deacon in the early Middle

---

[323]*Unitatis Redintegratio,* in Flannery, *Vatican Council II,* 488.

[324]Ibid., 496.

[325]Evangelos Theodorou, *Heroines of Love: Deaconesses through the Ages* (Athens: Apostoliki Diakonia of the Church of Greece, 1949); Evangelos Theodorou, *The 'Ordination' or 'Appointment' of Deaconesses* (Athens, 1954) (in Greek); Cipriano Vagaggini, "L'ordinazione delle diaconesse nella tradizione grèca e bizantina," *Orientalia Christiana Periodica* 40 (1974): 146–89.

Ages, the ordination of women to the diaconate was not prohibited.[326] From the Byzantine Middle Ages on, she writes, women deacons were chiefly found in monasteries. In modern times, the Russian Orthodox Church sought to revive the practice of ordaining women deacons in various ways. The Russian Orthodox priest and missionary to China Makarii Glukharev proposed a missionary order of women deacons in 1837 and 1838, a proposal not supported by the Russian Orthodox Synod. Even so, he did gather a group of missionary women who performed diaconal ministry. In 1860, at the behest of Grand Duchess Elena Pavlovna, sister of Tsar Nicholas I, Russian Orthodox priest Aleksandr Gumilevsky proposed creation of nursing deaconesses and of parish deaconesses, eventually gathering twelve parish deaconesses.

Efforts to revive the order of women deacons apparently continued, for by 1907 a Russian Orthodox Church commission reported deaconesses in every Georgian parish, ministering equivalently to today's catechists and Eucharistic ministers. Creation of deaconesses apparently continued elsewhere.

In the Greek Orthodox Church, a nun on the Greek island of Aegina was ordained by Bishop Nektarios, who was then criticized for ordaining a woman, but who is now recognized as a saint. FitzGerald reports that, since people were scandalized at the time, the Bishop then explained that her appointment was perhaps more characteristic of the subdiaconate. The nun did, however, wear the diaconal stole during the ordination, and the ceremony followed the proper formula. Up to the mid-1950s, nuns in various places in Greece became monastic deaconesses; some were ordained and some were not. Concurrently, in 1952 a college for "lay" (secular) deaconesses was established in Athens, which by 1990 had become a graduate school of social work training women to work as assistant pastors, with the hope expressed in its mission statement that the Church of Greece would in the future have deaconesses in parishes as well as in convents.

---

[326]For the historical data I rely primarily on K. K. FitzGerald, *Women Deacons in the Orthodox Church: Called to Holiness and Ministry* (Brookline, Mass.: Holy Cross Orthodox Press, 1998), 149–60.

Meanwhile, multiple inter-Orthodox conferences have discussed and in many cases put forth a call to return to a more general practice of ordaining women to the diaconate.[327] Specific consultations that have called for the restoration of the order of the deaconess include those in Romania in September 1976, and in New York in 1980. Most recently, the published report of the Interorthodox Symposium at Rhodes, Greece (October 30– November 7, 1988) states:

> The apostolic order of deaconess should be revived. It was never altogether abandoned in the Orthodox Church though it has tended to fall into disuse. There is ample evidence, from apostolic times, from the patristic, canonical and liturgical tradition, well into the Byzantine period (and even in our own day) that this order was held in high honor. The deaconess was ordained within the sanctuary during the Divine Liturgy with two prayers; she received the Orarion (the deacon's stole) and received Holy Communion at the Altar.
>
> The revival of this ancient order should be envisaged on the basis of the ancient prototypes testified to in many sources (cf. the references quoted in the works on this subject of modern Orthodox scholars) and with the prayers found in the *Apostolic Constitutions* and the ancient Byzantine liturgical books.
>
> Such a revival would represent a positive response to many of the needs and demands of the contemporary world in many spheres. This would be all the more true if the diaconate in general (male as well as female) were restored in all places in its original manifold services (διακονίαι), with extension in the social sphere, in the spirit of ancient tradition and in response to the increasing specific needs of our time. It should not be solely restricted to a purely liturgical role or considered to be a mere step on the way to higher "ranks" of clergy.
>
> The revival of women deacons in the Orthodox Church would emphasize in a special way the dignity of woman and

---

[327] In his prologue to K. K. FitzGerald's study, Evangelos D. Theodorou notes conferences in Agapia, Romania (1976), New York (1980), Chania, Crete (1990), Levadia, Greece (1994), Addis Ababa, Ethiopia (1996), Damascus, Syria (1996), Constantinople, Turkey (1997), Cambridge, N.Y. (1998), and Nairobi, Kenya (1998). See FitzGerald, *Women Deacons*, xxiv.

give recognition to her contribution to the work of the Church as a whole.[328]

The Armenian Apostolic Church ordains women to the diaconate.

The Armenian Apostolic Church is one of the Eastern Churches that did not accept (or did not attend)[329] the Council of Chalcedon (451) — the others being Syrian Orthodox, Coptic Orthodox, Malankara Orthodox, and Ethiopian Orthodox, from which the Eritrean Orthodox broke in 1993.

There are at least two recent declarations of unity between the Pope and the Supreme Patriarch of the Armenians, one between Paul VI and Catholicos Vasken I in 1970, and another between John Paul II and Catholicos Karekin I in 1996.

The Armenian Apostolic Church, which is recognized by Church authority as in the line of apostolic succession, has never abandoned its practice of ordaining women to the diaconate. The history of ordained women deacons in the Armenian Apostolic Church has been published and, while there are very few women deacons today, they do exist.[330]

A principal reason for retaining women deacons in the Armenian Apostolic Church is the requirement for a deacon to celebrate the liturgy of the Eucharist. The deacon at the Eucharistic liturgy has three main functions: (1) instruct the faithful, principally as to rubrics; (2) serve the celebrant; and, (3) read the Gospel. No one can be delegated to this office; the deacon must be ordained and must wear the stole during the liturgy. Typically, in women's convents and monasteries, a woman deacon would be ordained to provide for the liturgy. In modern times, up to World

---

[328]Ecumenical Patriarchate, *The Place of the Woman in the Orthodox Church and the Question of the Ordination of Women*, Report of the Interorthodox Symposium, Rhodos (Rhodes), Greece (October 30–November 7, 1988), ed. Gennadios Limouris (Katerini, Greece: Tertios Publications, 1992), 31–32.

[329]The Armenian Apostolic Church did not attend Chalcedon because of Armenia's involvement in war at the time. It officially rejected Chalcedon in 607, primarily due to pressure from the Byzantine empire.

[330]Abel Oghlukian, *The Deaconess in the Armenian Church: A Brief Survey*, trans. S. Peter Cowe (New Rochelle, N.Y.: St. Nersess Armenian Seminary, 1994).

War I women deacons were always nuns and served only in monasteries. Since World War II, women deacons have also served in
parish churches — in Constantinople they served in the patriarchal church in the center of the city — and one woman deacon
even visited the United States in recent memory and was asked
to serve in the liturgy in a few parishes in the United States. The
female deacon is a deacon ordained to major orders, equivalent to
the male deacon. While there is no rule against married women
deacons, there are solely celibate women deacons in the Armenian Apostolic Church at present. While some women deacons
reside in convents, they are not necessarily members of religious
orders.

The Church can return to the tradition of ordaining women to the diaconate.

Given that it already implicitly recognizes the fact of ordained
women deacons, the Church can easily return to that tradition.
The work of the Church, so varied and so presently demand-
ing of all who would take it up, is not changed substantially
from the work that called women centuries ago. Catherine of
Siena's desire to disguise herself as a man in order to enter the
Order of Preachers and devote herself to what has now become
known as the apostolic ministry of the Church is both chronicle
of her present and predictor of ours. Raymond of Capua's re-
counting of the conversation she had with the Lord echoes the
wish of other women, past, present and future, to serve the
Church.

> "Why are you sad," He asked her, "because I am now draw-
> ing you on to the work which you have longed for from your
> infancy?" She replied, "Lord, if it be not presumptuous, how
> can what you say be done? How can one like me, feeble and
> of no account, do any good for souls? My very sex, as I need
> not tell you, puts many obstacles in the way. The world has no
> use for women in such a work as that, and propriety forbids
> a woman to mix so freely in the company of men." The Lord
> replied with dispatch. "With me there is no longer male and

female, nor lower class and upper class; for all stand equal in my sight, and all things are equally in my power to do."[331]

The Lord's startling response brings hope even now. Women deacons already exist. As the permanent diaconate is more clearly defined, its place as an office of the Church through which both men and women can participate in the teaching, governing, and sanctifying roles of apostolic ministry will be better recognized.

While the question of the readmission of women to the ordained diaconate has long been one of legitimate public theological debate, despite and perhaps because of the arguments of those who argue that women were never ordained to the diaconate as we know it today and so neither may be admitted now, as the Church recognizes the validity of the sacramental ordination of men deacons in the Eastern Churches, so must it recognize the validity of the orders of women deacons. Therefore, there would seem to be no barrier to returning to the practice of ordaining women to the diaconate in the West.

In conclusion.

What Catherine of Siena did is what thousands of women do every day, yet there was and is no formal sacramental dimension to their ministry. If we agree that men and women are ontologically equal, then we agree that women can be ordained. Despite the determinations by Church authority, particularly where the iconic argument is culturally accepted, that women may not be ordained priests or bishops, there has been no determination that women cannot be ordained permanent deacons. The clear historical evidence that women have been ordained to service of the Church in the diaconate with precisely the same ritual as men is essentially challenged with the notion that women were not truly ordained because women cannot be ordained. The historical exegesis of holy orders necessarily includes the fact that there were deaconesses on the roster of clerics in the early Church,

---

[331]Raymond of Capua, *The Life of Catherine of Siena,* trans. Conleth Kearns, O.P. (Wilmington, Del.: Michael Glazier, 1980), 116–17.

and despite scholarship that seeks to convince Church authority and the People of God that women who were once ordained to the diaconate were not actually ordained — that there was some ceremonial recognition of their service without the conferral of a sacrament — it is clear that the matter (laying on of hands) and form (words) were observed.

As the ordination of women to the diaconate was once possible, so it is possible again. In fact, the Armenian Apostolic Church ordains women to the diaconate, and Church authority recognizes the validity of the sacrament of orders in the Armenian Apostolic Church.

The continued call of women to diaconal service by the Church, demonstrated by women's service in diaconal ministry with or without orders, underscores the fact that the ordained ministry of service by women is necessary to the Church, that is, to both the People of God and the Hierarchy. The determining factors are the needs of the whole Church and the ways in which those needs may be met.

Therefore, the matter is more clearly resolved in favor of the restoration of the female diaconate as an ordained apostolic ministry.

One can only hope in the Spirit.

Index

Abbesses, 103, 105
  in canoness institutes, 124
  juridical authority of, 107–9, 123–24
Abbeys, 109, 123–24. *See also* Canoness
  institutes
Acolytes
  vesting of, 153–54
  women as, 10, 73–74
Ad Gentes, 134, 162
Ad Pascendum, 131
Alb, 153–54
Allen, John L. Jr., 84n.138
Ambrosiaster, 103
Anglican Churches, 44
Anthropology
  ecclesiology reflecting single-nature,
    22–24
  God and Church limited by dual-
    nature, 29–31
  iconic argument against single-nature,
    24–27
  women's passivity in dual-nature,
    27–29
Apostles, 26, 30, 36, 50, 55, 57–58
Apostolic Canons of the Church, 156n.296
Apostolic institutes, 119–20
  freedom of movement by, 121–22
  Institute of the Blessed Virgin,
    120–21
  ordained female diaconate should not
    replace, 143
  Order of the Visitation of Mary, 122
"Apostolic Letter on Reserving Priestly
    Ordination to Men Alone," 56–58.
  See also Ordinatio Sacerdotalis
Arles, Council of, 108
Armenian Apostolic Church, 171–72
Augustine, 39

Austria, 83–84
Auxiliaries of the Apostolate, 162n.309

Backmund, N., 124n.233, 125n.236,
  126n.241
Baptism, 139, 168
  by a lay person, 158
  as sacramental remedy against sin, 42
  women forbidden from performing,
    104
  women performing sacrament of, 55,
    76
Beal, John, 150n.282, 155n.294
Beatrice of Nazareth, 115
Beben, Mary, 33n.50
Beguines, 113, 114–17, 146
Bernardin, Joseph, 52n.80, 81
Bevilacqua, Anthony J., 12n.19
Bible, 54–55, 57–58. *See also* Scripture
Bishops
  abbots/abbesses' preeminence over,
    107–8
  authority over women in ministry,
    17
  call for women deacons, 84–85
  early Church deaconesses and, 95,
    102
  power and jurisdiction of, 68–69,
    149–50
  on reasons for diaconate, 70–71
  restrictions on becoming, 65
  rights of diocesan, 11
Bobbio monastery, 108
Boulard, Marie-Odile, 125n.239
Boyer, Louis, 160, 164n.313
Bradshaw, Paul F., 37n.55, 68n.104,
  97n.172
Brockman, Norbert, 92

Canon 1024, 78–79
Canoness institutes, 124–27, 143
Canon Law. *See* Code of Canon Law
Canon Law Society of America, 85, 91,
    130–32
    on ordaining female deacons,
        161n.308
"Can Women Be Priests?" 54–56
Carthage, Council of, 104, 107n.202
Cassock, 154
Castrillón Hoyos, Darío Cardinal, 165
Catherine of Siena, 82, 113, 117–18,
    132, 172–73
Catholic Common Ground Initiative,
    80–81
Catholic Theological Society of America
    (CTSA), 61–62, 163
Chalcedon, Council of, 104–5, 108, 171
Christ
    diaconate dependent on, 133–34
    as exemplar of all humanity, 34–35
    men representing, 24–26, 40–41, 52
    women representing, 23n.38, 50–51,
        52–53, 55–56
Christ, Carol P., 30n.47
Chrysostom, John, 103–4
Church
    acceptance of iconic argument, 26–27
    Beguines as threat to authority, 116
    call for women deacons from
        contemporary, 83–86
    can return to ordaining women to
        diaconate, 172–74
    categories create separatism in, 6–9
    dual-nature anthropology limits,
        29–31
    function and nature of, 79–81
    gender relations in, 3–4
    as hierarchical, 4–5
    ordained female diaconate supports
        function of, 139–42
    ordained female diaconate supports
        stability of, 138–39
    ordained female diaconate responds
        to whole, 135–38

ordaining women to priesthood vs.
    diaconate in, 36–38, 64
recognizing authority to ordain
    women to diaconate, 162–66
reflecting single-nature anthropology,
    22–24
restricted possibilities for women in,
    9–11
retaining service of unordained
    women in, 142–45
understanding of priesthood in,
    65–67
women called to ministry in, 145–47
women fitting into function and
    structure of, 82–83
women ordained in Eastern, 168–72
women's juridical authority in, 107–9,
    147–48
women's participation in, 1–3
See also Church, early; Eastern
    Churches
Church, early
    controversy over women's ministry in,
        100–103
    diaconal ordination of women in,
        97–100
    four categories for women's ministry
        in, 111–12
    ordained female diaconate
        discontinued in, 103–7
    women deacons evidenced in,
        87n.145, 94–97
    See also Church; Middle Ages
Clergy. *See* Clerics
Clerics
    expulsion from clerical state, 12–13
    separatism and, 7–10
    sharing roles with, 6–7
    See also Ordination of women to
        priesthood; Priesthood
Code of Canon Law, 73
    on clerics vs. laity, 7–8
    on entering clergy, 54n.85
    on infallibility, 62
    on lay altar service, 73

on lay preaching, 151
on women religious, 11
on women's juridical authority,
147–48
Congar, Yves, 135n.260, 164n.313
Congregation for Institutes of Con-
secrated Life and Societies of
Apostolic Life, 8n.11
Congregation for the Doctrine of the
Faith, 47–48, 79, 148–49
on *Ordinatio Sacerdotalis, Responsum
ad Dubium,* 58–61
Congregation for the Evangelization of
Peoples, 45
Convents, 146n.274
Coptic Orthodox Church, 171
Council of Arles, 108
Council of Carthage, 104, 107n.202
Council of Chalcedon, 104–5, 108,
171
Council of Nicea, 67
Council of Trent, 38, 50–51, 109, 119,
157n.300
Council of Vienne, 116–17
Coyle, John K., 47n.71
"culture of equality," 22
Czechoslovakia, 56

Daly, Mary, 28–29
Daniélou, Jean, 101n.181, 111–12, 127
Davies, J. G., 95n.167, 96n.168, 97n.173
Davis, Barbara, 162n.309
Day, Dorothy, 82
Deaconesses
as clergy, 67
vs. deacons, 37, 83
discontinuation of ordaining, 103–7
early Church evidence of, 94–97
early Church ordination of, 97–100,
101–2
evidence found in Scriptures of, 93
four categories of ministry by, 111–
12
as separate order in early Church,
74–75, 76–78

use of term, 90–92, 104
See also Diaconate; Ordination of
women to diaconate
Deaconesses: An Historical Study, 92–93
Deacons
compared with deaconesses, 37,
76–78, 90–92, 95–98
duties of, 158–59
marriage and, 9–10
vs. religious and secular women, 17
See also Diaconate; Ordination of
women to diaconate
de Chantal, Jane Frances, 113–14, 122,
132
Decree on the Apostolate of Lay People,
152
DeLambo, David, 160nn.305–6
De Langogne, Pie, 123nn.229–30
Delooz, Pierre, 82n.133
de Noronha, Galvào, 75n.120
de Sales, Frances, 122
de Vitry, Jacques, 114–15
Diaconate
calling forth to, 68–71
clerical state through ordination to,
157–58
contemporary Church calls for
ordination of women to, 83–86
deaconesses vs. women ordained to,
83
does not lead to priesthood, 92
fading of male, 87
iconic argument does not apply to,
43
as ministry of service, 71–72
priesthood distinguished from, 18–19,
37–38, 65–68, 141–42, 155–56
restoration of permanent, 133–35
See also Deacons; Deaconesses;
Ordination of women to diaconate
Diakonein, 90
Didascalia Apostolorum, 95–96, 131
Dierks, Sheila Durkin, 33n.50
D'Oignies, Marie, 114–15
Dulles, Avery, 25–26, 30, 62n.98

Eastern Churches
  apostolic succession in, 167–68
  women ordained in Armenian
    Apostolic, 171–72
  women ordained in Orthodox,
    168–71
Ecclesiology. *See* Church
Eisen, Ute, 87–88n.149
English Ladies, 120–21
Epaon, Synod of, 105
Episcopal Church, 44
Epitome of the Apostolic Constitutions,
    98–99
Ethiopian Orthodox Church, 171
Eucharist
  all female services for, 33
  iconic argument and, 26
  maleness as implicit to priesthood
    and, 42–43, 53–56
  See also Sacraments

"feminine soul," 28, 33
Feminists, 30, 31–32, 137–38
FitzGerald, Kyriaki Karidoyanes, 89–90,
    94n.161, 168–69
Foley, Nadine, 127n.243
Ford, J. Massyngberde, 88n.148, 90
Forget, J., 96n.169
Fransen, Piet, 151n.285
Francis of Assisi, Saint, 65, 115

Gaudium et Spes, 46
Germany, 84–85
Gertrude the Great, 113
Glukharev, Makarii, 169
God
  dual-nature anthropology limits,
    29–31
  as male vs. female, 30–31
  See also Christ
Goddess, 30, 31
Gottemoeller, Doris, 130n.250
Greek Orthodox Church, 169
Gregory VII, Pope, 125
Gregory XIII, Pope, 119

Gregory XV, Pope, 121
Groer, Hans Hermann Cardinal, 84
Gryson, Roger, 91, 92–93, 96n.170,
    98–99, 101nn.180–83, 102–4
Gumilevsky, Aleksandr, 169

Hardy, Edward R., 157n.300
Hebblethwaite, Peter, 163–64
Hefele, C. J., 103n.188, 104n.192,
    105n.196, 106n.198, n.199, n.201
Hennessey, Paul K., 108n.205
Hildegard of Bingen, 113
Hill, Christopher, 46n.98
Homily, preaching by lay persons,
    151–52
Honorius I, Pope, 108
Hugh of St. Victor, 38–39

Iconic argument, 103
  applying to diaconate, 161
  opposing ordaining women to
    priesthood, 24–27, 43–44
  symbolization of Christ in, 55–56
Ignatius of Antioch, 18n.32, 97
Innocent III, Pope, 123, 125
Institute of the Blessed Virgin Mary,
    120–21
Intercongregational living, 146
Inter Insigniores, 45–46, 47n.71, 49–56,
    64
  applying to diaconate, 65
International Theological Commission,
    5, 45, 66, 75n.120, 163–64
International Women's Year, 44, 46

Javierre Ortas, Antonio M. Cardinal,
    74n.116
Javorova, Ludmila, 56n.89
Jermann, Rosemary, 47n.71
Jesuits, 120–21
Joan of Arc, 82
John XIII, Pope, 125
John XXII, Pope, 117
John XXIII, Pope 46
John Paul I, Pope, 45–46

John Paul II, Pope, 45–46, 47
  on "culture of equality," 22
  on women's church participation, 1–3, 8
  on women's equality to men, 23–24
Johnson, Elizabeth A., 23n.38, 82n.133
Julian of Norwich, 113, 118–19, 132
Juridical authority
  of abbesses, 107–9, 123–24
  in canoness institutes, 124
  by lay persons, 148–49
  restriction on women's, 147–48, 150

Kalsbach, A., 91n.156, 101n.181
Kane, Sister Teresa, 12n.19
Kay, David J., 108n.205
Kelley, John, 141n.268
Kempe, Margery, 113, 118–19, 132
Knox, John, 109n.207

Langley, Wendell E., 47n.71
Laodicea in Phrygia, Synod of, 103
Law, Bernard Cardinal, 62n.98, 155–56
Lay ministers
  juridical authority of, 148–50
  ordaining, 81–82
  performing functions of deacons, 156–57
  preaching by, 6n.6, 151–52
  sharing roles with clerics, 6–7
  women as, 10
Lay ministry, 72
  clericalization of, 81, 160
  distinguishing diaconate from, 160–61
  ordained female diaconate should not replace, 143–44
  preferred over ordained female diaconate, 139
  restrictions on women in, 73
  training, 15–16
  See also Women in diaconal roles
le Begue, Lambert, 114
Lectors, 73, 153
Lee, Elizabeth Meredith, 114n.213

le Guillou, Marie-Joseph, 79n.125
Lehmann, Karl, 84–85
Le ministère des femmes dans l'Église ancienne, 92–93
Leo XIII, Pope, 11n.18
Les diaconesses: Essai historique, 92–93
Liège, Diocese of, 114, 115
Liftin, Alice I., 14n.25
Ligier, Father Louis, 45
Liturgical ministry, 119–20, 153–54
Lobinger, F., 81n.131
Lucius III, Pope, 125
Lumen Gentium
  the Church defined by, 79–80
  on diaconate, 139–40, 159
  on laity, 7, 83n.135
  on ordination to priesthood, 71n.113

McCann, Dennis P., 6n.5, 142
McDonough, Elizabeth, 147–49
Malankara Orthodox Church, 171
Mansour, Agnes Mary, 12n.19
Marliangeas, B. D., 135n.260
Marriage, 9–10, 65, 104–6
Martimort, Aimé Georges, 75n.21, 91, 92–93, 97–98
Martos, Joseph, 67n.103, 77n.122
Mary, Mother of Jesus, 27–28
Massey, Marilyn Chapin, 29–30
Mayer, Josephine, 46n.69
Mechtilde of Magdeburg, 113
Meier, John P., 47n.71
Men
  Church controlled by, 3–4
  denial of women's freedom and power by, 28
  in lay ministry, 15–16, 73
  as lectors/acolytes, 153n.288
  ordination of married, 65
  possibilities for church participation, 9–10
  religious institutes of, 127–28
  restoring permanent diaconate for, 133–35

Men (*continued*)
    symbolizing Christ, 24–26, 40–42, 52
    women as equal to, 22–23, 34–35
    See also Deacons; Priesthood
Menstruation, 74
Meyer, Octave, 126n.240
Middle Ages, 65, 132
    ordination of women during, 168–69
    women in diaconal roles during,
        113–19
Milligan, Mary, 121, 129n.247
Milner, Helmut, 125n.238
*Ministry of Women in the Early Church,
    The,* 92–93
Monasteries, 107–9, 113, 123–24
Morris, Joan, 108n.203, 109n.206,
    125n.235
Morton, Nellie, 30n.47
Mother Teresa, 82, 136
Mulieris Dignitatem, 26nn.41–42
Murnion, Philip J., 160nn.305–6
Murphy, Caryle, 33n.50

National Conference of Catholic
    Bishops, 134, 135n.259, 164n.316
Nicea, Council of, 67
Notre Dame de Saverne, 125–26
Nuns, 143, 169
Nygren, David J., 130n.250, 144n.271,
    145n.272

O'Connor, John Cardinal, 70n.110
Oghlukian, Abel, 171n.330
O'Neil, Mary Aquin, 22n.35
Orange, First Synod of, 104
Order of the Visitation of Mary, 122
Origen, 89, 101n.184
Ordination of women to diaconate
    arguments against, 18–19, 74–75
    calling forth to, 68–71
    Canon 1024 on, 78–79
    Canon Law Society on, 85, 130–32
    ceremony for, 37n.55, 67–68,
        74n.118, 97
    Church can return to, 172–74

    Church recognizing authority over,
        162–66
    closing priesthood to women does not
        preclude, 36–38
    contemporary Church calls for, 83–86
    cooperation with Church ministry,
        155–58
    vs. deaconesses, 77–78, 83
    debate on historical evidence of,
        92–93
    distinguished from priesthood and lay
        ministry, 71, 158–61
    in early Church, 97–100, 101–2
    early Church discontinuation of,
        103–7
    ecumenical interests and, 167–68
    function of the Church and, 79–81
    juridical authority by abbesses
        following, 107–9
    menstruation and, 74
    as ministry of service, 71–72
    permanent relationship through,
        13–16
    preaching of homily and, 151–52
    questions on, 65–66
    responds to needs of whole Church,
        135–38
    should not replace unordained
        service, 142–45
    supported by history and scripture,
        87–90
    supports function of the Church,
        138–42
    supports stability of the church,
        138–39
    See also Women in diaconal roles
Ordination of women to priesthood
    arguments against, 24–27, 42–44,
        49–58
    church documents on, 45–48
    discussion closed on, 62–63, 64
    discussion on, 44–45, 58–63
    infallibility of teachings over, 59–62
    vs. ordaining to diaconate, 64

Ordinatio Sacerdotalis, 47–48, 56–58, 64, 65
  reply to, 58–61
Orléans, Second Synod at, 105
Orsy, Ladislas, 48n.72, 61
Orthodox Churches, 93, 168–72
Osiek, Carolyn, 34

Papal congregations, 128
Paul VI, Pope, 44, 45, 131, 134, 149, 171
Pavlovna, Elena (Grand Duchess), 169
Permaneder, M., 98n.175
Peter Lombard, 39–40, 41–42, 42n.62
Phoebe, 74–75
Pius V, Pope, 119
Pius XII, Pope, 41, 50–51, 121, 149
Polycarp of Smyrna, 100n.179
Pontifical Biblical Commission, 54–55, 57–58
Pontifical Commission on the Study of Women in Society and in the Church, 44
Porete, Marguerite de, 116
Power, David N., 8n.12
Priesthood
  diaconate as distinct from, 18–19, 37–38, 65–68, 141–42, 155–56
  early Church deaconesses moving to, 97–98
  maleness as implicit to, 42–44
  not all deacons eligible for, 92
  See also Clergy; Ordination of women to priesthood
Prioresses, 123–24
Provencher, Normand, 47n.71

Quedlinburg Institute, 124–25

Radegund, St., 105
Rahner, Karl, 79n.125
Rand, Laurence, 75n.120
Ratzinger, Joseph Cardinal, 58, 59, 60, 75, 149, 164–65
Rausch, Thomas P., 45n.67

Raymond of Capua, 118, 172–73
Rescripts, 18, 69n.108, 148, 150n.281, 152n.287, 157n.298
Responsum ad Dubium, 58–61
Reynolds, Nancy, 130n.251
Reynolds, Philip Lyndon, 47n.71
Romania, 170
Ruether, Rosemary Radford, 33, 136
Russian Orthodox Church, 169
Ryan, J., 108n.203

Sacramental ordination, 102, 133–34
Sacraments
  in history of deaconesses, 77, 94–95
  open to all persons, 38–40
  persons symbolizing Christ and, 40–44, 50–53, 55–56
  priesthood's relation to, 36
  See also Eucharist
Saints, 82, 93
Scripture
  on Church's function, 80
  evidence of women deacons in, 88–90, 93
  See also Bible
Seasoltz, R. Kevin, 108n.205
Second Vatican Council, 7, 14, 55–56, 66, 131, 143, 158, 168. *See also* *Lumen Gentium*
Secular canonesses, 124–27
Sepe, Crescenzio, 164
Sexism, 3–4
Sharkey, Michael, 5n.4, 66–67nn.101–2, 164n.313
Skillen, Harmon, 130n.251
Smith, Callistus, 11n.18
Society of Jesus, 120–21
Spiritual directors, 16
Stiefel, Jennifer H., 89
St. Mary's, Überwasser, 125–26
St. Ursula's, Cologne, 125
Subsidiarity, 142
Sylvester II, Pope, 125
Syrian Orthodox Church, 171

Teresa of Avila, 82
Tertullian, 98n.175, 100–101
Theodore I, Pope, 108
Theodorou, Evangelos D., 98, 168,
    170n.327
Thomas Aquinas, 50n.76, 51n.79, 53
Thomistic systematic theology, 23
Tilley, Terrence W., 115n.215, 154n.292
"Tradition and the Ordination of
    Women," 61–62
Trent, Council of, 38, 50–51, 109, 119,
    157n.300
Trinity, as male, 34–35

Ukeritis, Miriam D., 130n.250,
    144n.271, 145n.272
Union of International Superiors
    General, 128–29
Unitatis Redintegratio, 167

Vagaggini, Cipriano, 98, 163–64, 168
Vatican II. See Second Vatican Council
van Lunen-Chenu, Marie-Thérèse,
    44n.63
Venerable Bede, 108n.203
Verbi Sponsa, 123–24
Vienne, Council of, 116–17
Violet, Arlene, 12n.19
Virgins, order of, 101, 102–3, 105,
    143
Visitandines, 122
Vita Consecrata, 8, 11

Ward, Mary, 113–14, 120–21, 132
Weiland, J. Sperna, 5n.4
Widows, 102–3, 143
    appointed vs. ordained, 101
    confused with deaconesses, 99–100
    as deacons, 104
    early Church order of, 96
Winninger, P., 135n.260
Wir sind Kirche, 84

Wittberg, Patricia, 130n.250, 137n.264
Women
    called to Church ministry, 145–47
    church participation by, 1–6, 14–15
    controversy over early Church
        ministry of, 100–103
    fitting into Church function and
        structure, 82–83
    as lay persons, 8
    ontologically equal to men, 22–24,
        34–35
    organizations of, 32–34, 136–37; see
        also Apostolic institutes
    passivity in, 27–29
    restrictions on church participation
        by, 9–11
    restrictions on juridical authority by,
        147–48, 150
    serving as acolytes, 73–74, 153n.288
    speaking in religious services, 106–7
    training for ministry by, 15–16
    vesting of, 153–54
    See also Deaconesses; Feminists;
        Ordination of women to diaco-
        nate; Ordination of women to
        priesthood; Women in diaconal
        roles
Women in diaconal roles, 113–14
    apostolic institutes, 119–23, 127n.243
    Beguines, 114–17
    Catherine of Siena, 117–18
    church retaining unordained, 142–45
    Julian of Norwich, 118–19
    Margery Kempe, 118–19
    modern, 127–30
    secular canonesses, 124–27
    strengthened by ordination, 133–35
    See also Lay ministers; Lay ministry
Woolf, Virginia, 32
Woywod, Stanislaus, 11n.18

Zagano, Phyllis, 115n.215, 154n.292